The Barge Buyer's Handbook

A step by step guide to buying a barge

The Dutch Barge Association Ltd 1998

Researched, written & published by

The Dutch Barge Association Ltd

Port Werburgh, Vicarage Lane, Hoo, Kent ME3 9TW

Phone 07000 BARGES (07000 227437)
Fax 01932 765734

Website www.barges.org
E-mail info@barges.org

1998 The Barge Buyer's Handbook
Second edition

This handbook has been produced by the joint efforts of DBA members. Our grateful thanks go to everyone who has contributed to the creation of the book, for writing and proof reading, for additional material and corrections, for photographs and illustrations, for design and production, and to Rolf Stricker who gave his time and expertise for the actual production. Profits from the sale of the handbook go to the DBA and help to support the work of the Association.

Edward Burrell, Chairman
May 1998

Changes and mistakes

We have done our best to ensure that all the information in this book is correct. However, as we deal with hundreds of details, it is possible that an error has occasionally slipped in. Do please let us know of any errors you notice. As every reasonable care has been taken in the preparation of this book, we can accept no responsibility for errors, omissions, or damage, however caused.

ISBN 0 953281 90 6

CONTENTS

INTRODUCTION

Many people have found buying barges difficult. Most buyers have learned a lot from the venture, particularly from first purchases, and would do it better or at least differently another time. We felt it worthwhile to try to give you the chance of avoiding some pitfalls by letting you benefit from the experience of your predecessors.

We have been able to collect this experience largely because of our Association, which attracted the many contributors to this book. The Association's aims are to bring together barge enthusiasts, to work with other organisations with compatible aims, and to communicate on behalf of our members with navigation authorities and other official bodies. Many members own barges, others are dreaming of doing so, some are 'just looking'.

The Association was formed because of a need for an organisation for those interested in the sort of craft not always welcome at the yacht club. While its name is 'The Dutch Barge Association', it welcomes those interested in any type of barge (or indeed any inland craft wider than a narrow boat). It matters not whether the vessel is a Humber keel, Leeds & Liverpool short boat, Polish tug, German torpedo recovery launch, or luxe motor.

We make representations to authorities on matters such as maintenance of waterways for barge traffic, navigation charges, and barge 'driver's licences'. We organise rallies regularly, both in England and elsewhere, and our branches hold their own local social gatherings. We have a growing number of contacts with businesses involved with barges in a commercial or professional capacity, very useful for sourcing equipment peculiar to barges and for advice and discounts. We also publish a quarterly magazine, *Blue Flag*, which contains much useful technical and other factual information for present and potential barge owners, and relays interesting and amusing experiences to give members some of the feeling of what barging is all about.

This may sound like an advertisement, which it is to some extent, but it also leads to the first serious piece of advice to the prospective barge owner. Join us. You are almost bound to find support and help available through the Association to be very valuable. If nothing else, it will introduce you to people sympathetic to your problems.

So welcome to our *Barge Buyer's Handbook.4* We hope you find it useful, whether you are buying a barge or already own one. However, a couple of provisos: this handbook contains the work of a number of people who inevitably have some differences of opinion, so contrasting views have been included where they suggest a range of sensible choices. And while reasonable efforts have been made to ensure the accuracy and appropriateness of the handbook, the Association cannot take responsibility for its contents or for omissions. Always try to confirm the information for yourself.

If you have questions, please do not hesitate to telephone us at
07000 BARGES (07000 227437).

SUMMARY OF CONTENTS

This handbook is organised into chapters to match the topics most people have to deal with as they approach barge ownership. This may be a logical order but it will not necessarily be the sequence you follow. Barge buying is not that tidy!

1. It starts with answers to the question you will almost certainly be asked early in the game, 'Have you taken leave of your senses?'.

2. You will soon discover how varied barges are. What should yours be like? We take you through the crucial process of deciding what you are looking for, and help you decide what characteristics you want your barge to have.

3. Only when you have a picture of the barge you are after can you really decide whether you can afford it. No, not the purchase price (that comes in the following chapter). Here we take you through the real expense: the costs of owning a barge.

4. In case we have not frightened you off by now, we go on to describe the market for barges. What might you expect to find for sale, and at what prices?

5. Few barges used for pleasure are less than 50 years old, so condition is a vital consideration. We make suggestions as to what you should look for during your first viewing, introduce the all-important survey, and discuss the various other documents you should expect to see.

6. Your search can then begin in earnest. We cover where to look, and how to work with brokers.

7. Because you may end up buying your barge in another country, we take you through the purchase transaction in some detail. This includes how to negotiate it, what commitments the parties are making, what paperwork is needed, and details of the survey.

8. Finally, when you have bought your barge, then what? We end with some ideas on getting it home, particularly if you have never steered anything larger than an outboard runabout before.

We include in the Appendix a short bibliography, a checklist to help you through the process, and a list of contacts you may find useful.

Don't worry if this all sounds daunting. Thousands of people have gone through the process successfully, and there is no reason why you should not do so too. But do be prepared for a few experiences which may later result in amusing stories in the bar (or the wheelhouse).

1 YOU WANT TO BUY A *WHAT?*

Although your acquaintances may not think so, there are several very
sensible reasons for owning a barge:

- It can be one of the most comfortable and manageable craft for cruising.
- It can make a commodious and unique home.
- It can be an absorbing interest, with a fascinating sense of history.

And, in all these aspects, it can be surprisingly cost-effective.

Of course, there are also some negative points. We will get to them too.

1.1 CRUISING

We assume you are already aware of the delights of the inland waterways.
However, if you are familiar only with routes in the UK, you have the
enormous joys of the huge mainland Europe network to come.

A major advantage of a barge for inland cruising is that you get a lot for
your money. The vessel is likely to have much more space than anything else
most of us could conceivably afford. Moreover, since weight of goods on
board is not a problem, a barge can readily include all mod. cons. (a typical
barge can carry at least 50T; you are very unlikely to have more than 5T of
domestic possessions). It can literally be a home away from home.

Barges are tough. They were designed to take the knocks of inland freight carrying, so they can easily take pleasure travel in their stride. If you have navigated in a conventional pleasure boat, you will find the lack of worry about occasional grounding or glancing contact with navigation works a great relief. If damage does occur to a barge, repairs to its steel work are usually much less costly than equivalent work on a fibreglass or wooden craft.

Barges are much easier to handle than you might expect. Why this is so becomes clear when you think about their history. Barges are, or were, business tools, devices for carrying freight at a profit. They were designed and evolved to do this efficiently, which meant not only having as much room inside as possible for their size (for freight) and being able to move through the water while consuming as little fuel as possible, but also being able to be run by as few crew as possible. This has resulted in the right equipment being incorporated, carefully designed and located to do the jobs needed with minimum effort. The outcome is that most of the types of barge we are interested in can be navigated readily by two ordinary people, and can even be moved successfully by one person at a pinch.

1.2 RESIDENCE

The shape of most barges allows them to become a convenient and space-efficient residence. They are very stable on inland waters (which means, among other things, they do not tip when you step on board), and most can safely take the ground on a drying tidal mooring.

It is not all rosy, of course.

Mortgages for barges are less easily available and usually attract higher interest rates than those for houses. Also, finding any acceptable residential mooring, let alone a charming one with secure tenure, can be a significant problem, especially in Britain. Although a barge can be just as cosy as a modern house, a badly converted one can be damp and chilly.

But many have found that once they have lived on a barge they cannot imagine why they ever had a house or flat. There really is something very special about it, despite the occasional hassle.

1.3 HERITAGE

At larger boat shows you can see brand new replica barges on sale (we do not use 'replica' unkindly – just to indicate that these craft never carried freight). For many purchasers, this is the ideal answer: they are happy to pay a (sometimes hefty) premium for the peace of mind of a new hull and new equipment.

However, most of us buy ex-working vessels. Few of these were built after the 1920s in the popular sizes and some are over one hundred years old. Yes, this raises immediate worries about maintenance and condition, but it also gives the craft very special and individual character and interest.

The barge vendor will often be able to tell you, usually with some pride, about his vessel's history – where it worked, what it carried, who its crew were, what unusual things happened to it. But if he cannot, there are people who specialise in tracing barge histories with the same zeal that others use in filling in a family tree. It feels good to know that your barge used to take tulips to the flower market, or even stront (the Dutch word for a certain natural product) out to fertilise the fields.

As with all antiques, the design and construction of barges varies very widely, and there is much debate about which features are most useful, clever, or beautiful. And the subtle (or not so subtle) marks of an honourable working life can give today's owner the warm feeling of a link with earlier days.

You may decide to look for a barge with particular historic features, or keep or change those your vessel happens to come with. For instance, is the single-cylinder engine which you have to start with a blow lamp your idea of owning a piece of industrial archaelogy, or will you replace it instantly with a modern diesel?

2 WHAT SHOULD YOUR BARGE HAVE?

Most barges were designed for specific traffic and routes. With a whole continent of extensive inland waterways, it is not surprising that they vary enormously. Although this choice may seem overwhelming at first, it is actually an advantage as it gives the buyer the chance to find exactly what he wants.

The key initial question is probably size: we explore this topic in some detail below. Aesthetics must also be heeded, so we cover the various styles; also 'motor vs sailing' (if you want real horse power we will have to leave you to it). We end this section with considerations of the quality of the conversion and accommodation, and some thoughts on doing your own conversion.

2.1 EFFECTS OF SIZE

Barges come in many sizes. Although it may be possible to change any of a barge's dimensions (*more on this below*), it is a lot cheaper not to. Getting one that is already the size you want is definitely a good idea. But what is that size? Answering this question is something you should spend considerable time on before buying.

Size is a major determinant of cruising range, accommodation, costs of ownership (mooring and maintenance in particular), availability of moorings, availability of dry docks, and regulations. Perhaps surprisingly though, the purchase price does not necessarily grow with the barge because above a certain size barges get less desirable for leisure use.

2.1.1 CRUISING RANGE

The main consideration limiting your choice of size may be where you want to go with your barge. The bigger the vessel, the fewer inland routes it will fit. Be realistic. You may never brave the potentially treacherous Irish Sea with a craft designed for quiet inland waters, so why limit your vessel's length to that of the locks on the Grand Canal between Dublin and the Shannon?

Navigation gauges vary as much as barge sizes. Although many waterways were built to one of several 'standard' gauges, there were a lot of local initiatives too, so it is hard to generalise. The best approach may be to familiarise yourself with the waterways map (*see Appendix II*) and with waterway dimensions for your hoped-for cruising range, and then to decide which routes you are prepared to forego if you want a bigger vessel.

We include a table of waterway gauges but with some important reservations. The table (p. 14) gives maximum length and beam (width) for most routes listed, and you can usually approach these limits with some confidence.

You also need to consider draft (the depth of the water) and air draft (the clearance above the water). For these dimensions, more caution is advised. It is too easy to get stuck in poorly dredged or rubbish-filled channels, or under low bridges when water levels are high. In practice, you will almost certainly be glad you allowed a generous clearance above and below.

Officially quoted waterway dimensions can be misleading. Fortunately, they tend more often to be conservative than optimistic, except in the all-too-frequent cases of dredging arrears. Sometimes the actual gauge is surprisingly larger than the official one, especially in Britain. There are some counter-examples, though: in the UK some bridges are reinforced with sprayed concrete, reducing the width to below the official dimension, or (on arched bridges) reducing the width at which the official air draft applies. If a dimension is crucial, ask around – get opinions based on recent local experience.

Air draft is probably the most awkward dimension. It is significantly affected by bridge and vessel shapes, and is virtually impossible to specify accurately for many routes given the variations in bridge design.

The only sure solution is to seek informed local knowledge and to measure key bridges yourself. To do this, identify both the lowest flat bridge and any notoriously tight arched ones. An arched bridge can be checked quite easily by measuring the headroom every 30cm or so across the bridge hole with a plumb line. Do not forget to note whether the water is up to its normal level. If the towpath passes under the bridge, record how far it sticks out. A minimum bridge cross-section can then be drawn and compared with a scale drawing of your intended vessel's cross-section. (We would like to know your results please.)

You may wish to cruise in the British Isles as well as in mainland Europe, so the table covers principal waterways there. It excludes the extensive network of English narrow boat canals, which accept craft up to 2.1m wide only. It does include, however, some barge navigations which are derelict at present but which may return to life while you are a barge owner.

British barge waterways are both varied and small in European terms. They have developed very little since they were originally built. UK size constraints increase as you move inland from tidal waters. The maximum comfortable draft is not much over 1m if you want to venture off main rivers, and 0.9m is better. Even on such routes as the Thames, exceeding 1.2m may limit your range and pleasure. You will start to cut your cruising range seriously with an air draft of more than 2.1m (with the wheelhouse down), particularly if you have a wide superstructure at that height. The Kennet & Avon navigation, a major east–west route, cannot take any more than that, the Thames above Oxford not much more, and the arched bridges on the Grand Union Canal, a major north–south route, are definitely unpleasant for barges much taller.

At present, the UK barge navigations are divided into regional networks in the south, east, and north connected by narrow canals which could be widened, derelict barge navigations which could be restored, or unnavigable rivers which could be opened. Several projects to create such links are at various stages of progress at the moment, so inland barge cruising from one end of the UK to the other may become a possibility in time.

The table *(see page 14)* includes the majority of the French waterways, but leaves out a number not connected to the main network and omits such narrow oddities as the Canal de l'Ourcq and the (largely derelict) Canal du Berry.

If one foregoes access to the British rivers and 'wide' canals, the next effective size constraints are the dimensions of some routes in France which are sub-Freycinet. The (full) Freycinet dimensions are a standard introduced in the nineteenth century by a French minister of transport (*Monsieur Freycinet, bien sûr*), who set the following standard gauge for the French waterways (dimensions in metres):

Length	38.5
Beam	5.0
Air draft	3.5
Draft	1.8

Most French and Belgian waterways were upgraded to this standard after the 1880s, and subsequently most barges using them were built to these maximum dimensions. But some waterways and some barges were not. A Freycinet-gauge barge is often called a 'péniche' in France or a 'spits' in the Low Countries.

Waterways isolated from the main network, such as those in Brittany, tended not to be rebuilt to the Freycinet standard. There were also some notable exclusions within the network for various historic reasons, some of which you may well want to use. The principal ones are the Canal de Bourgogne, Canal du Midi, and Canal du Nivernais.

A fixed air draft of 3.5m will in theory allow travel almost anywhere in France – but sometimes only with great care. 3.4m will give much greater peace of mind. A demountable wheelhouse reducing air draft to no more than 2.7m gives the most flexibility.

Within reason, we suggest the less draft the better. *(But see the discussions under Accommodation and Handling below).*

The table does not include waterways in the Netherlands, as routes of almost every size exist there, originally designed for vessels carrying from 5T through to over 24,000T, and often (and still being) upgraded. In general a Freycinet vessel will get to enough Dutch places to satisfy most people. However, check the sizes of the smaller canals if you hope to ditch-crawl up charming tiny routes. The standard reference work on them is the *Almanak voor Watertoerisme*, published by the ANWB, the Dutch tourist board. It is quite understandable to anglophones even though available only in Dutch.

2.1.2 ACCOMMODATION

It is an iron rule that no matter how large a vessel you buy, you will eventually wish it had more space inside. You will at various times want more berths, more storage, more room for equipment, or a squash court (not necessarily a joke – we know of one barge with a front-garden size lawn on the cabin top, and another with a swimming pool).

There is also the question of hold depth. Barges were built with differing sizes of hold to allow for such factors as density of freight to be carried and the depths of waterways used. In the larger sizes, holds can seem vastly deep: two-storey (or deck, if you must) conversions are possible.

If one storey will do, a reasonably shallow hold is often more suitable. You are then likely to be able to see out of the windows while you are standing on the floor inside or even sitting at the dining table. This can be achieved in a deeper hold by building the floor well above the bottom of the vessel *(but see further comments below on this technique)*. Otherwise, you may have to depend on skylights for light, and these often leak or drip condensation.

Freycinet-gauge barges are widely available at the moment, and the large volume of space they offer can be tempting. However, many people find they really do not need this much space, the holds are too deep, and a barge this big is just too much of a good thing. Very commodious accommodation can be built into something considerably smaller.

WATERWAY GAUGES

Waterway	Length	Width	Draft	Air Draft
British Isles				
Avon River (Stratford)	21.34	4.11		
Basingstoke Canal	21.34	4.11		
Calder & Hebble Navigation	17.53	4.27		
Chelmer & Blackwater Navigation	18.29	4.27	0.65	
Forth & Clyde Canal (Scotland)*	21.18	6.00		
Grand Canal (Ireland)	18.59	3.96		
Grand Union Canal (London–Braunston)	23.47	4.25		
Grand Union Canal (Braunston–Birmingham)	23.47	3.84		
Grand Union Canal (Trent–Foxton)	21.94	4.25		
Huddersfield Broad Canal	17.53	4.27		
Kennet & Avon Canal	21.34	4.22		
Leeds & Liverpool Canal	18.90	4.27		
Lee, River	25.90	4.87		
Nene, River	21.34	3.96		
Ouse, River Great (Lower)	21.34	3.81		
Ouse, River Great (Upper)	21.34	3.20		
Ouse, River Yorkshire (Lower)	18.29	4.27		
Ouse, River Yorkshire (Upper)	17.37	4.27		
Sheffield & South Yorkshire Navigation	18.75	4.27		
Shropshire Union Canal (Ellesmere Port–Nantwich)	21.34	4.01		
Stort, River	25.90	4.06		
Thames & Severn Canal*	21.34	3.80		
Trent & Mersey Canal (Preston Brook–Middlewich, Trent–Burton)	21.34	4.23		
Wey & Arun Canal*	21.34	3.51		
Wey, River	22.40	4.23		
France				
Brittany Waterways	25.00	4.60		
Canal de Bourgogne	38.50	5.05	1.80	3.10
Canal du Midi	30.00	5.50	1.60	3.00
Canal du Nivernais	30.15	5.05	1.00	2.70
Freycinet Standard Waterways	38.50	5.05	1.80	3.50

All dimensions are in metres.

They are best guesses only. No guarantees.

* Wholly or partly unnavigable as we go to press.

We have mentioned demountable wheelhouses before. You can indeed increase your cruising range, but you will soon be fed up with putting it up and down if you have to do it too often. Demounting is particularly disruptive if you use the wheelhouse as your (fully furnished) living room. So a lower air draft when the wheelhouse is up is worth considering.

The overall layout of the accommodation is important. Some conversions keep the separation of fore-cabin, hold and wheelhouse, so you have to go outside to pass from one to the other. Think about making that trip in winter or in rough water. Others have stairs from the wheelhouse straight down into the hold accommodation, and an internal door into the fore end.

Open-plan gives space and light

2.1.3 HANDLING

Most barges handle well, due to their stability and large rudders. But the bigger the barge and the smaller the waterway, the more challenging the navigation. The skill needed increases rapidly as any one of a vessel's dimensions approaches a route's size limits. A full-gauge barge (such as a Freycinet barge on a Freycinet waterway) will travel quite slowly because water must squeeze through the small gaps left between barge and masonry or silt. Having a bit of clearance to spare can make life much easier.

Putting two storeys in a barge requires a lot of ballast if the cabin top is to fit under bridges. The now much heavier barge is correspondingly trickier to manoeuvre and also harder to stop. Its added momentum gives it much greater capability to do serious damage if it hits something it should not. It is also deeper so more likely to run aground. As a result, many feel the two-storey approach tends to result in a barge too ponderous for general pleasure cruising. Perhaps it is better to leave it to the hotel péniches.

Similar considerations apply to a single-storey craft with a deep hold. You may still need a lot of ballast to help the barge get a grip on the water when you are trying to stop or make a turn. The space under the floor can be used for tanks, spare furniture, wine cellar, etc. but nonetheless conventional wisdom gives preference to a shallow hold and a modest draft.

Finally, there is handling at sea to consider, especially if you plan to do anything more than a dash across the Channel. Some, but not all, larger Dutch barges were built for both inland and estuary work, and occasionally as seagoing craft. They have stronger frames and a more marine shape than their strictly inland counterparts. Spits are seldom suitable for the sea, as they were usually designed for inland use only. Their shapes are bluff, their construction is light, their plating is thin. Some have been known to break in the middle when taken into the sort of rough water which can be found even in such inland bodies as the Ijsselmeer (formerly the Zuider Zee).

2.1.4 OWNERSHIP COSTS

We go into ownership costs in more detail later, but some thought should be given to them here.

There is no getting around it. Owning a big barge costs more than owning a small one, even though the bigger one may be cheaper to buy.

Mooring is a key consideration. Mooring costs vary with length, whether the space is purchased, leased or rented. You may not need a permanent mooring initially, or for some time. You can cruise through the Netherlands, Belgium and France for years, never staying in one place for more than a few months, and incur negligible mooring charges along the way. However, in the end, most owners decide they want a base and the feeling of security it can bring.

Bigger boats cost more to maintain. Think of all the extra painting! Slips and dry docks tend to charge by the metre, and surveyors by their time (they can test the thickness of only so many square metres of bottom in an hour).

Many navigation authorities levy charges (licences, vignettes) which vary with size, some even with multiples of dimensions, e.g. length x beam. Our Association considers this unfair, as few of the authorities' costs vary with craft size, but getting them to abandon this practice is proving a long battle.

2.1.5 REGULATIONS

Most nations consider a barge above a certain size to be a ship, and start applying ship-like regulations. These can include onerous registration and safety equipment provisions, and requirements that the skippers must have professional credentials. Some of these rules (such as some related to steerers' qualifications in France and the Netherlands) come in at boat lengths as little as 15m. British registration becomes more complex at lengths of 24m plus.

2.1.6 CHANGING THE SIZE

What if you just cannot find a barge of the exact size you want? It happens, particularly if your search time is unavoidably short. Well, you could consider changing one or more dimensions of a barge which is the wrong size.

Many barges were lengthened in the past to increase capacity, and these can be good prospects for shortening since this may restore the proportions and curves lost in the lengthening process. Some barges shorten well as they have uniform cross sections over a considerable length. We know one spits which was very successfully shortened from 38m to 24m, leaving just the original forward and after accommodation, the engine room, and a small hold between for a workshop. However, do not forget that shortening does not reduce air draft or the depth of the hold, so not all shortcomings of a large vessel can be dealt with in this way.

Similarly, a barge with a relatively constant cross-section can often be lengthened without much difficulty. This is more expensive than shortening, as a new section must be built. If you do opt for lengthening, it may be best to have the work done in the Netherlands. Yards there are used to this type of work, while managers of those in the UK tend to start muttering and multiplying cost estimates by large factors when you suggest such a project.

One DBA director's barge started its career a bit longer (and was shortened) and a bit wider (and was narrowed by pruning its wide rubbing bands) than he wanted. It was also too high, necessitating removal of the fixed wheelhouse and substitution of a demountable one, and too deep, so some ballast had to come out. The necessary surgery rendered it just the size he was after, but soon after it was done the owner saw a beautiful vessel for sale with exactly the right dimensions!

So are you after a clog-sized tjalk, or a Freycinet gauge spits? Make up your mind before you start looking. Be warned, though. Despite all the science, immediately after you decide your specifications you are all too likely to fall in love with a barge with all the wrong measurements (we will avoid the obvious analogy here). Only you can deal with that problem.

2.2 TYPES OF BARGE

We will talk in detail about only British and Dutch barges. This is not because we are biased – it is just that these are the only nationalities of barge you are likely to come across in the size you want. There are a few rare exceptions. For example, one DBA member was offered a 21m by 4m German river patrol vessel, which had the interesting advantage of an all-aluminum superstructure, but he was put off by the thought of replacing the two huge diesels which gave it a 50km/h pursuit speed with something better suited to pottering.

We will also limit ourselves to metal (iron or steel) craft. Wooden barges are few and far between now because they are so difficult and expensive to maintain.

2.2.1 BRITISH

Almost no barges for inland work have been built in Britain since the 1950s, and very few are still in trade now.

English barge waterways comprise a collection of canal and river navigations mostly grouped around the Thames, Severn, Mersey or Humber.

Each area evolved its own varieties of craft. The principal types you might still find are the Leeds and Liverpool Canal short boats (but very few are left) and the Yorkshire keels. A good many ex-sailing or motor keels still exist.

English barges have a reputation for toughness. Keels, for example, were designed to trade on the north-eastern waterways, many of which are tidal, and typical standard form was (and still is) to race down the Trent on the ebb until there was too little water left to float in. The vessel would then rest on its chosen shoal with the crew slumbering until the grating of gravel on the bottom signalled the flood and time to get up and get moving again. Obviously, the vessels needed to be strong to survive this type of regular treatment.

Keels were built to a very bluff and quite deep design for maximum capacity, and to a number of standard sets of dimensions.

The short boats are basin-shaped craft, with shallow hulls. A craft of similar size, but slightly different character, developed on the (southern) Irish canals, and a number of these can still be found, some unconverted.

Other types of British barge which occasionally crop up include ex-coasting ones (such as the famous Thames sailing barges, which fit in almost none of the UK canals), the vanishingly rare Norfolk wherries, and various varieties of Mersey, Weaver and Manchester Ship Canal barges.

Most English barges were run by shore-based crews as opposed to families living on board, and were owned by carrying firms. These craft were working implements only, and as such were usually not subject to much of the loving care bestowed on the family-run long distance narrow boats or most Dutch vessels. For this reason, many English barges, while very rugged, tend to show neglect, evidenced by pitted metalwork, numerous dents, and significant internal hull and frame corrosion.

In many ways these battle scars form part of the character of the vessel and add to its appeal, but equally they can make conversion and maintenance difficult indeed.

A Leeds and Liverpool short boat

2.2.2 DUTCH

The Netherlands has been riddled with barges for several centuries; every area developed its own types and hybrids. They came in all sizes, upwards from tiny vessels for poking up field drains to collect crops.

However, since the 1950s, the Dutch government has intervened in an attempt to make the barge trade more economic. It offered to buy, at attractive prices, small barges still carrying. It scrapped many it bought. It also offered compensation to owners of barges to take them out of freight-carrying and convert them into something else, which is one reason for the many barge houseboats in the Netherlands. Overall, this means that there are very few unconverted small Dutch barges still around.

Dutch barges were in general much more lightly built than English ones. It was not normal for ships to take the bottom fully loaded. The waterways were more often of uniform uncluttered depth, and capacity took precedence over strength. Whereas standard plating thickness for a 50T Yorkshire keel would be 10mm, a 250T Dutch luxe motor would be built in a mixture of 6 and 8mm plating. The Dutch vessel's frames would be closer together but much smaller than in the English counterpart.

For this reason, allowing a Dutch barge to take the bottom regularly on a drying mooring requires caution. Soft mud does little harm, but hard uneven river bottoms do stress a hull, particularly where wash or wave conditions cause jarring as the vessel settles and rises on each tide. The wooden Thames sailing barges could dry out with a high degree of impunity, sometimes taking up alarming shapes but springing back to normal as soon as they floated. A Dutch barge will flex too, but not necessarily fully resume its previous shape afterwards.

Selection of bow shapes

On the other hand, many Dutch craft have been family-owned and run, and the subject of fanatical pride. This shows in their condition. Deterioration through internal corrosion is rare on a boat which recently traded, or at least it will be confined to isolated and usually predictable areas. Any dents sustained were normally ironed out rapidly before other skippers noticed them. Of course, examples of poor maintenance exist, and some Dutch barges used for day-boat gravel haulage etc. suffered as a result. It is worth checking a craft's history if possible.

Older conversions are often poorer because inadequate rust prevention precautions were used inside the hull. Because plating is generally thinner, neglect more rapidly takes significant toll. Never buy a run-down and dented

Dutch barge unless the price is really, really cheap, because there are lots of better ones out there. The costs of repairing deformed bows, tatty decks and peeling rubbing strakes can be very high relative to buying a good hull in the first place.

All Dutch barges have their individual characters which can never be recreated in a new vessel. Nevertheless, there is a small trend now towards new replica Dutch motor barges, both in England and the Netherlands. The Dutch have been building replica sailing vessels for years, but turned to motor ones only more recently. A replica offers the reassurance of a modern welded hull, with massive frames and thick plating, so it can take the bottom and bounce through bridge holes with impunity. Below the water line, the hull form may be more simply shaped than a riveted original, as this is a cheaper way to build.

So much for the principal differences between British and Dutch craft. Now to enter the minefield of the classes of Dutch barge. Beware, you are at last about to be exposed to some Dutch terminology.

The Dutch do not have a generic name for inland craft which equates to 'barge'. The nearest is *'binnenvaartschip'* – inland transport ship (as opposed to *'grotevaartschip'* or deepwater ship). Although English has more terms for barge types than most people might think (wherry, short boat, hopper, Tom Pudding, pan, lighter, keel etc.) the Dutch have far more than the Brits do. Dutch craft are usually named according to one or more of four parameters: shape or style, size, area of origin, or function. We will start with some general descriptions of common styles.

Aak

Take a fairly parallel-sided marrow, cut it in half lengthwise, keep one half, and scoop out all the flesh. Put it on the table and squash it down a bit so the bottom is fairly flat and each end is slightly higher than the sides. Now you've got the basic shape of an aak (and a very messy inedible marrow).

At the back, you need to put a small triangle standing vertically, forming a slightly raked sternpost to hang the rudder on. Give it fore, aft and side decks set down a little from the rim of the shell, and hatch coamings standing up to form the hold opening. Set a mast at the front of the hatches, and lee boards each side. Possibly add a bowsprit, and then give it cutter rig with the mainsail on a gaff and boom.

Some aak variants are hasselteraak, ijsselaak, zandaak, rijtaak, and hagenaar. Nor should we forget the Dorstense aak, the keen or the herna. However, you probably should not worry too much about this for now – it is more like the difference between an MGTD and MGTF for car enthusiasts.

Some examples of hull shapes, British and Dutch.

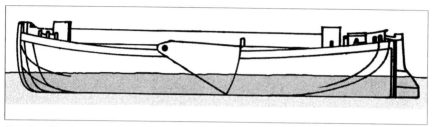

Humber Keel

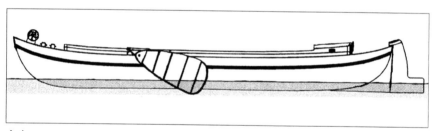

Aak

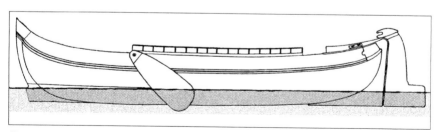

Tjalk

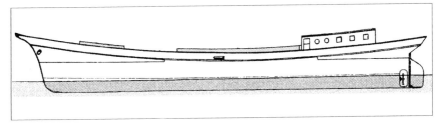

Klipper

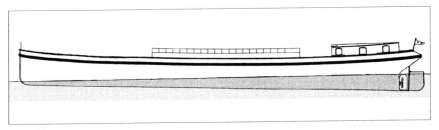

Katwijker

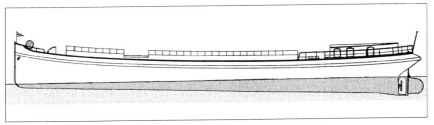

Motor barge, such as Steilsteven, Beurtschip, Luxe motor

Hagenaar

The hagenaar is an example of a craft named for its area of origin – Den Haag. The size of the hagenaar was determined by the 4.20m wide Wagenbrug ('brug' means bridge in Dutch) at Den Haag. This is a common beam for Dutch craft. Luckily for those wanting to cruise in Britain, it is just narrower than the somewhat standard 14 ft beam of many UK 'broad' locks.

Tjalk (pronounced 'chal'k')

Take your aak and raise the deck to the top of the shell. Add a stem post and give it new bulwarks which lean inwards slightly, especially at the front and back. You should have a thing that looks more or less like a clog – that is your basic tjalk. Your lifesize one will probably be more heavily built than the aak.

There are various types of tjalk. The paviljoentjalk, for example, has lovely stern cabins with sternward facing windows.

The westlander is named for its province of origin. Originally built of wood, westlanders were used to carry fruit and vegetables, but also sand, stone and manure. A westlander looks something like a tjalk with its bow pushed slightly in. They are generally small barges, which loaded 10–40T.

For detailed descriptions of these and other types, we refer you to Martens & Loomeijer in their book '*Binnenvaartschepen*' (Uitgeverij de Alk bv, Alkmaar, 1977). Yes, of course, it is written in Dutch, but there is a recent book in English, *Dutch Barges* by David Evershed, which covers the sailing varieties.

Tjalk types often offer a good potential for a spacious conversion in the smaller sizes, since a larger cabin, if sympathetically built, can more easily be in keeping with the original style. However, the smaller sizes will also tend to have been out of trade for a longer time, implying a longer period in private ownership and perhaps therefore a longer period of neglect.

Klipper

Take a tjalk and press the sides of the fore-end so it is more pointed, then make the stempost and bulwarks flare out rather than lean in: you have got the beginnings of a klipper or klipperaak (nothing's straightforward with barges).

Klippers may come with one or two (or even three) masts. Again there are sub-types: noordzee-klipper or schoeneraak, and klipperaak, etc.

Steilsteven

The word means 'straight stemmed', and these barges do indeed have vertical stem posts. The steilsteven stern is rounded and similar to that of an aak, but the curves are less extreme. As with the aak, there is usually no structural stern post, with, as for the aak bow, the keel plate simply carrying on up to the deck. An external sternpost is fitted to carry the rudder, and latterly the propeller.

Overall, steilstevens have particularly subtle and elegant lines and are highly prized ships. They originated as sailing craft in Friesland and Groningen provinces and were often engaged solely in the sugarbeet and potato trade, being tied up for the rest of the year. They were much easier and cheaper to build than a tjalk or aak, without losing any carrying capacity. They might be engaged solely in day trade, or fitted with a luxury stern cabin. Sometimes they had both motor and sails, and particularly heavily built versions were made for working in the North and Baltic seas.

The types described above were almost all originally sailing craft. As such, they are often more satisfactory for work in more exposed waters; some types were specifically built for trading at sea. However, the Dutch tidal estuaries and the Ijselmeer are shallow, and conditions in such waters can deteriorate very rapidly and impose substantial demands upon any vessel. And do be careful – the presence of a sailing rig on a barge does not indicate its capability to handle blue water.

Luxe motor

Many Brits fall in love with luxe motors, which is fortunate because most Dutch prefer more traditional craft and think luxes are a bit nouveau and so do not bid their prices up quite so much.

The luxe motor was among the first of the purpose-built motor barges and may be considered an evolution of the steilsteven. Most date from the 1920s. A luxe motor usually has a proper engine room separated by full bulkheads, and superior stern living quarters which often were wonderfully fitted with varnished wood and etched glass.

They vary greatly in size, from 15m to 38m or more.

The luxe motor hull usually has a sweeping counter stern (which reminds some people of the Titanic) and a straight stemmed bow.

Beurt(motor)schip

Beurtschip means literally 'regular ship', a functional name describing vessels engaged in a regular scheduled service, particularly around Friesland, as opposed to the more common bulk cargo carriers. They were originally built as tjalks, and eventually as a variant of steilsteven and then luxe motor.

These were the workhorses of Friesland. They usually have a fairly small wheelhouse more or less right at the back. The accommodation was originally in the bow, with an entrance and skylight in the fore-deck, and sometimes a small porthole in the hull plating to give further light and ventilation. They mostly had a single hold, and a mast (derrick, really) sprit-rigged on the fore-deck for self-discharging.

The fore-end bulwark (the small fence usually found around the bow above deck level to stop you falling off the front, and sometimes along the sides and back as well) commonly continues with a tubular toe rail where it joins the fore-deck; there is often a similar rail about 30cm high around the stern-end coming forward as far as the rear bollards next to the steering position.

They usually lacked the saloon roef (stern cabin), being used as day boats on regular scheduled runs. A flat stern deck took its place.

They were generally motor craft, and loaded from 50T to 250T. Many beurt-motorschips have finished up as bunker boats, little tankers serving ships and bulk cargo vessels – further definitions by function.

Katwijker

Another popular type, this is named after the town of Katwijk which had a particularly low bridge with an air draft of 1.80m. This forced the Katwijker to have a very shallow hold, a low wheelhouse, a horizontal steering wheel (many have since been replaced by vertical ones), a gear lever with a remov-able top, and a bow the top of which could be unbolted and removed, all to reduce air draft. The other obvious distinguishing feature is a very wide rubbing band all round the gunwale, originally of timber clenched in metal although the timber has long since rotted away in most. This is ideally suited for hanging up the barge on the lockside as the water level drops!

2.2.3 A NOTE ON SEAWORTHINESS

Most luxe motors and similar motor barges will hold their own at sea in calm weather conditions, usually with a maximum stipulation of force 4. However, even in force 3 or 4 winds, or even less if there is a chop, motor barges can roll very uncomfortably if they take waves on the beam.

These barges can make coastal journeys in suitable weather, but only if properly prepared, and if the skipper (or his pilot) has the necessary skill, knowledge and judgement. But they should not be thought of as sea-going craft. A lot of extra time must be allowed for any barge sea trip as you must wait for the right weather. You should never be driven to sea by impatience – supported by hope that the wind will drop, or not rise, after you leave port.

2.3 SAIL OR MOTOR?

You can see from the types of barge described that many were originally built to sail, or were derived from sailing designs. Furthermore, there are now quite a few successful conversions to sail of luxe motors, which as their name suggests were not originally intended for wind propulsion.

In fact, barges sail surprisingly well, being manoeuvrable, easy to handle (the Thames spritsail barge had a crew of one man and one boy), and steady. Because most have leeboards (drop keels on each side of the hull), sailing does not prejudice their shallow draft. They can be unexpectedly fast. Try a day on the Humber in 'Comrade' or 'Amy Howson', particularly in a stiff breeze. These are a restored keel and sloop respectively, and are available for charter. You may be amazed how an apparently square chunk of iron can charge along with only the wind for power.

Barges which sail are readily available on the market. They have many advantages (the challenge of sailing, the silent progress, the beauty of the rig). However, do not let that blind you to their disadvantages. They have all the capital and maintenance costs of a motor barge plus those of the rig. Although the masts of most are counterbalanced and can be lowered quickly, the rig can get very much in the way if you want to take them inland, and is often best removed from the barge and stored on the bank somewhere safe when you leave wider waters. And you usually have to demount any wheel-house (which, in fact, many sailing barges do not have) when you are sailing, fully exposing you to the weather. We do not want to discourage you from buying a sailing barge, but do urge you to make a realistic estimate of how often you would actually sail, as opposed to motor, before you decide.

One last thought. Barges which originally sailed may not work under power as successfully as vessels designed to motor. Many tjalks, for example, are shallow draft with rounded hulls, and side slip considerably on corners and in windy conditions. You may find you need to use the lee boards for adequate control in some circumstances. Also, the shape of these hulls can make it difficult to install a bow thruster (*see below*).

2.4 EQUIPMENT

To a newcomer to the scene, a barge seems to contain a large and bewildering collection of unfamiliar and often greasy apparatus. This tends to generate an unpleasant feeling. You know that all this stuff is probably essential. But you barely know what it does, let alone whether the barge you are looking at has all the necessary bits, whether anything vital is missing and may need to be purchased expensively later, whether the bits which are there carry respected brands, and whether they are in good enough condition.

There is no easy answer, and even those more familiar with barges can be confronted with types of equipment they have never come across before, made by manufacturers they have never heard of. Even a long-term owner might not be able to find his way around other engine rooms, particularly those representing several layers of marine engineering archaeology and the combined efforts of a number of previous 'practical boat owners'. And, of course, each barge owner has his own views about what is necessary and what can be dispensed with – views likely to be influenced by what is in the barge he is trying to sell to you.

Cheer up, though. We will take you through the basics, which should at least arm you with some of the right questions to ask as you peer into an engine room full of strange-looking machinery. It will not take as long as you might think to gain confidence.

2.4.1 ENGINE ROOM

Even if you want a totally immobile barge, you may still end up with the remains of an engine room, so this seems to be the place to start.

You will soon see that it is not only the engine that lives in the engine room. You will often find all sorts of other pieces of equipment there to do with pushing the barge through the water, as well as machinery for generating electricity and heat, and various other features from storage shelves to work benches. Never think that once you have seen one engine room you have seen them all. Barges were not usually built according to detailed plans in the first place, and have often been altered since birth, so their engine rooms tend to be as individual as their previous owners, and may give you an interesting lesson on the history of the vessel. Although the excellent design and immaculate condition of the accommodation may impress you, the engine room may reveal a totally different aspect to the ship.

A motor barge tends to have a purpose-built engine room. It is usually easy to enter and spacious, with standing headroom, due to the fact that the original engine of maybe 15kW probably took up four times the space as does the more modern 90kW machine now ensconced. Typically the original engine room was a space between two watertight bulkheads in front of the aft cabin, or between a bulkhead and the stern of the barge. In either case, this may have made it difficult to reduce its size when a smaller machine was fitted later, as moving a watertight bulkhead is not something you do in an afternoon.

In a sailing barge, space simply had to be found when an engine was added. In some cases the whole aft space under the deck was used. In others, the engine was put ahead of the original aft accommodation bulkhead and a second bulkhead fitted ahead of it to make a watertight engine room. In either case, the headroom may be restricted, and can even be as low as the engine itself, giving more of an engine space than a room.

Service work and repairs are obviously more easily done in a spacious engine room where you do not have to crawl through small holes, develop a hunch back, or lie in the bilge to do the job. However, other considerations creep in.

Your equipment may require less frequent maintenance than that built in the early 1900s. And you probably want to use as much as possible of the space on board for your accommodation. A big engine room may seem a bit wasteful in this light. It is possible to provide reasonable access to all the necessary machinery in quite a small space if it is well laid out, but sadly this has not always been achieved in non-original engine rooms.

When you are cruising, the engine room is the place where the noise and fumes are created. It is a good idea if you can keep them there: a fully isolated space is an advantage. This enhances fire safety too. Also, the ship's engineers need to get in and out of the engine room at times under way, when it is dark, the ship is rolling and the engine is running. So access should be convenient and wide enough, and your part of the engine room well lit and clear of hot exhaust pipes and bits of moving machinery.

A final point to consider when looking at the engine room architecture is what happens if you have to get the engine out of its home. How easy is it (or is it possible at all) to lift it straight out with a crane? Can you get it out with all its accessories fitted or will you first need to dismantle it partially in place and take the gearbox off (no fun at all)? In some cases ambitious owners get carried away with their conversions, and when the engine needs an overhaul they first have to cut away chunks of pretty steel work and demolish whole galleys, bathrooms, or whatever.

THE ENGINE

In most cases, you will want a barge that moves under its own power, so let us deal with the engine itself.

Barge engines are almost invariably diesels. Diesel engines are well suited to this purpose because of their greater durability compared to petrol (gasoline) engines, their fuel economy, and their limited need for electrical accessories like the spark plugs etc. of petrol engines.

You may be surprised at how small barge engines are. Even a 30m vessel may have only a 90kW unit (one horsepower is 0.75kW). A 20m vessel may happily get by with half that. This is because it takes unexpectedly little energy to move a barge through the water, particularly at walking pace – which is the normal top speed. In fact, even engines of these sizes are usually just loafing along during the average cruise as they now may have to shift as little as 10T of conversion, furniture and passengers as opposed to the 100T of cargo which they used to carry.

For a barge with a typical conversion used for cruising on average inland waters (not, for example, the Rhine at Koblenz), the minimum engine size required can be roughly estimated using the following rule of thumb:

$$\text{length (m)} \times \text{beam (m)} \times 0.75 = \text{power required (kW)}.$$

The main reason for having this much power is in case you need to stop or turn in a hurry, although it does not always work out that way. Some of the old barge masters may get along with only 30kW in the engine room, but they tend to know more handling tricks than do most of today's leisure skippers. An added safety margin of power makes good sense.

You might think that a more powerful engine would be much thirstier than a small one, but in fact the amount of fuel used relates more closely to the amount of work done than to engine size. Most barges burn something like four to five litres of diesel fuel an hour at normal speeds (under 10km/hour), no matter what engine they have.

Almost every type and make of diesel engine has been put into some barge somewhere, so you will come across a varied selection. They can be broken down into the following categories.

2-cylinder, air start Deutz, c.1936

a. Vintage

The first engines were put into barges over 90 years ago, and some of them are still running just fine. These were typically physically large (e.g. 7-litre) machines, very slow running (perhaps 600 revs/minute maximum), and not very powerful (some as little as 15kW) but with a lot of torque. They were simple and built to last. And they do. Such an engine often has one huge vertical cylinder. They are almost always water-cooled. Manufacturers of such engines which you may come across include Kromhout, Deutz and Klöckner. (UK canal boat enthusiasts may realise we are talking about something similar to a large equivalent of the Bolinders found in narrow boats.)

However, these engines lack refinements we take for granted with modern machines. For example, early engines were often semi-diesels, which means they can run only if they are hot. To start one from cold means playing a blowlamp over the top of the engine for 10 minutes or so then turning it over (often by hand or by foot). As a result, once going, they are kept running all the time unless the vessel is going to be tied up for a couple of hours or more.

It is quite feasible still to run a barge with such an engine. It adds a special character to the vessel, and its engine room can be the owner's pride and joy. However, as we have already suggested, these are large machines and take up a lot of valuable space, and will be under-powered for some waters; they are less convenient than modern engines and require more attention to run. Although more spare parts may be available than you might expect, you may have to have some specially made to fix a breakdown. On the other hand they are reliable and seem likely to last forever, and nothing can match the sound of their slow exhaust beat.

Some of these engines have no electrical accessories at all but a mechanical starting system powered by compressed air. An air-pump recharges the air bottle once the engine is running. This type of system is fine but its plumbing may look a little daunting.

We do not want to put you off a vintage engine, just to make you aware of what having one might entail.

The modern bargee and the classic boat enthusiast in you might run into a conflict of interest should you find one of those artefacts of industrial history in the boat of your desire. You just want to be able to turn the key and leave the wharf ... but would you rip out an original Boxer engine from a 1960 Porsche to replace it with a Suzuki 3-cylinder just to have a unit for which you can get spare parts easily? If yes, before you scrap the old lady, get in touch with somebody who might give her a new home. Museums and enthusiast clubs are often happy to take them in, or to help find someone who will.

b. Classic

The next age of barge engines brought the first true diesels (no blowlamps here). They, too, are big heavy machines but usually with two or four cylinders. They are also slow running, but not nearly as slow as the semi-diesels. They started appearing in the 1920s, and their era virtually drew to an end in the 1950s (although some are still made). They are more powerful than vintage engines – but not necessarily a lot more.

They, too, are usually water-cooled.

They are somewhat more sophisticated than the vintage engines, but may also have primitive features. For example, some have electric start but others must still be started manually. The spare parts situation is similar to that of the vintage engines: you may need to become a member of the enthusiasts' organisation for the brand of engine concerned.

PARSONS

OIL and PETROL

ENGINES

These engines are gaining the same degree of cachet that the hot-bulbs have had for some time. They are machines with a following, and can add to the atmosphere of your craft. But the same provisos apply to them as suggested earlier for vintage engines.

c. *Modern*

'Modern' engines may be 30 or more years old (if such an engine is well maintained, it should be able to withstand the relatively light demands of powering a barge for a very long time).

These are still 'industrial' engines, but more sophisticated than the classics. They will usually be four or six cylinder units, with maximum turning speeds of 1,800 to 2,600 rev/minute.

Most are water-cooled, but you may come across an air-cooled one.

There are many acceptable brands, from those more familiar to people in the UK (such as Cummins, Ford, Lister, Perkins, and Mercedes-Benz) to others more common in mainland Europe (such as Deutz, Hanomag, Industrie, Kromhout and Scania).

Some think the very best were (and still are) made by Gardner, a UK company. Gardners have a reputation for very high quality, particularly durability and fuel economy. They have been built in numerous sizes and configurations over the years. Some have been made under licence in the Netherlands by Kromhout.

But beware! Parts may not be interchangeable between the English and Dutch versions.

In the last 25 years or so, it has became common to use engines taken out of road vehicles. In the Netherlands, the overwhelming favourite was the DAF 6-cylinder, with power ratings from 65 kW to 80 kW. There is nothing essentially wrong with this approach, provided the engine has been properly marinised and installed. However, the engine may have been (much) used on the road before it came aboard, so a careful assessment of remaining life is in order. Common engines like the DAF may be bigger than really needed. A major advantage of this style of engine is that parts can often be found in road vehicle wrecking yards.

d. New (to you)

The barge you love may have a completely hopeless engine, or even none at all. This need not necessarily rule out a purchase. Install your own.

The easiest way to get an engine is to go to any manufacturer or supplier of marine engines, buy everything you need off the shelf and get the supplier to install it. Easy, but you may be looking at £10,000 to £15,000 for a 6-cylinder unit. On the other hand, you could get a truck engine, have it reconditioned and marinised by a specialist marine engineer who will probably be more than happy to install it for you as well. This could set you back between £3,000 and £7,000 depending on work and parts required. Finally, you could buy a used marine engine and overhaul it for between £2,000 and £5,000.

ENGINE INSTALLATION

An engine for a barge must first be made suitable for use afloat, a process called 'marinisation', then properly installed in the vessel.

Marinisation involves adding the necessary bits to an engine to enable it to work in a ship. There can be more to this than you expect. The essential elements are a cooling system and a connection between the engine and the drive (gearbox, propeller shaft, etc.), but there are other things which (some) engines need – such as instruments, special exhausts, fuel systems, starters, alternators and heavier flywheels. Some engines even need new oil pumps and sumps because they are mounted at different angles in boats from trucks.

A marine engine should, by definition, arrive already professionally marinised. An engine originally in a road vehicle, however, will have had the marine equipment added later, with potential for things to have gone awry. As often in life, there is an important difference between a proper job and bodging. You can often spot the latter quite easily by looking at the general state of fabrication and the quality of the components. Some have even retained the former truck cooling fan and radiator! But others are more difficult to detect, where the key bits are the ones you cannot see. Some DIY marinisations are done well, but beware those cobbled together on the cheap.

COOLING

There are two basic ways of cooling the engine: air and water.

A few Hanomags, Listers and Deutzs are still around which use large fans to blow air round the engine (although 99% of propulsion engines in barges are water-cooled these days). An air-cooled engine does not need as much pipe work, it avoids the risk of freezing up in winter and – most usefully – does not have raw water inlet filters (which are liable to get clogged and allow over-heating). On the other hand, these engines are noisy and they heat up the engine room. Also, they need to draw cool air from the outside, requiring air ducts and shrouds round the engine. These tend to clutter up the space and can make access difficult for engine maintenance.

Water-cooling comes in several variants. The most primitive uses direct raw water: water in which the barge is floating is drawn in through a hull fitting, pumped through the engine and then dumped overboard. Although this system does work, the water may not be the cleanest (and certainly will not contain anti-freeze) so is not really recommended.

A better approach is indirect cooling, where the raw water passes through a heat exchanger which fulfils the same role as the radiator in a car. The engine coolant (which should have anti-freeze in it) is inside the heat exchanger, and goes round the engine in a separate sealed circuit.

Another variant is skin tank cooling, in which no external water is drawn inboard. The heat exchanger is a large flat tank welded on to the inside of an underwater section of the hull: heat escapes through the hull. With this system it is vital to have a sufficiently large cooling surface area, and proper baffles in the hull tank. However, if the tank is too small, a second can normally be added without too much difficulty if there is enough spare and accessible hull surface inside. Unfortunately though, it is quite difficult to install a skin tank succesfully in a riveted hull due to the hull's irregular surface

Finally, to keel cooling. The skin tank is replaced by a heat exchanger comprising pipes immersed in cool water outside the hull. But these can be vulnerable and may pose a problem in shallow waters or on a drying mooring. More sophisticated is an open-sided steel box, smaller than a skin tank and let into the hull, inside which is a finned heat exchanger immersed in raw water.

It is usually possible, and need not be too expensive, to change the water cooling method (but not from air to water!). You can convert from direct to indirect, but if you plan to do so remember to budget for it in the purchase cost.

EXHAUST

Yet again you will find alternative ways of dealing with a requirement, in this case getting your exhaust fumes overboard.

The principal choice is between wet and dry. (No, this is not like the sandpaper that works both ways.) Either approach is acceptable.

A dry exhaust is like those used in cars. The exhaust gas goes out of the engine (manifold) into a pipe, through a muffler (silencer), and out through a hole in the hull or through the deck into a vertical stack.

The wet exhaust uses the raw engine cooling water after it has cooled the engine. This is injected into the exhaust pipe to cool the gases. It uses a different type of muffler, often rubber.

Dry exhausts are simpler, but are much hotter and so require insulation (lagging) to prevent injury to the crew and too much heat in the engine room. They also tend to be noisier than wet ones. On the other hand, a wet exhaust requires a water supply, so it may not be sensible to install this type if the barge has air or keel cooling. It also requires more maintenance (it may need draining for winter lay-up to avoid freezing). It must be installed so that water cannot siphon back from outside the hull and flood the engine – or even sink the vessel. And if the water supply fails (i.e. clogs), that nice rubber muffler may melt.

ENGINE INSTRUMENTS

Engines need instruments so the steerer can keep in touch with what is going on, out of sight, in the engine room. In some barges originally built for sail, the instruments are very inconveniently located and you may not even be able to see them when at the helm. Not a good thing. Other instrument panels may be very sparse. At minimum you need a tachometer, running hours meter, temperature gauge and oil pressure gauge. High temperature and low oil pressure warning lights and alarms are very worthwhile. A fuel gauge is handy (but often absent). There should at least be a volt meter for each DC electrical system. The instruments should have lights for night operation. The engine stop control should be very convenient to operate in case of emergencies.

MOUNTING

There are two main choices in installing an engine in a barge: solid or flexible mounting.

With solid mounting, the engine feet (part of the marinisation) are bolted straight on to the engine bed (heavy steel members usually welded to the hull). The advantage of this is that once everything is lined up and bolted down, it is nearly trouble-free. The disadvantage is that the engine vibrations and noises travel down the mounting into the hull. Most vintage and classic engines have to be on solid mountings.

Flexible mounting is used to reduce the noise. The engine feet sit on (relatively) soft blocks, which themselves are bolted to the engine bed. This does reduce vibration transmission, but unavoidably allows the engine to move about somewhat. To allow for the movement, there must be some kind of joint (there are several types) in the propellor shaft, usually incorporating a thrust bearing, and a flexible bellows in the exhaust system. This is a more complicated approach but the noise reduction can be worthwhile. Unfortunately, we are talking dynamics here and you may still get strange noises and even damaging vibrations at certain speeds. These often require an expert to remedy.

A final consideration relates to the environment. You rarely find a dry engine. They always seem to drip oil or diesel. Even if yours is completely dry, it is almost guaranteed that you will spill some oil during a change or some diesel when bleeding the system. This will dribble down and collect at the lowest point. If this is the same point where bilge water collects (such as the small amount which always drips through even a healthy stern gland, for example), there is a problem as the resulting mixture must not be pumped overboard. Ideally, there should be a drip tray under the engine. However, many older installations do not include one, and it can be very awkward to put one in after the act. In that situation, the bilge under the engine should be separated from the rest of the bilge by a bulkhead or dam. Today's regulations require one or other of these approaches.

FUEL SUPPLY

Engines need fuel, and there are important considerations here.

First, what type of fuel? Diesel is used almost universally. But there are two types: red (which is dyed) and white (which is colourless). White is about three times as expensive as red because its price includes road tax. This is what trucks use. Barges, like farm vehicles, used to be allowed to use red almost everywhere but there has been a growing trend throughout Europe to insist that pleasure vessels use white. Today, in the main European barge territory, only the UK and Belgium still allow red to be used. However, in most countries, this rule applies only to fuel used for propulsion. Red may still be used for heating or electricity generating.

This means that your barge should have two fuel tanks, one for red and one for white. If it does not, do not rule it out. Adding extra tanks is not that difficult provided there is room.

Tanks are usually made of steel and left untreated on the inside. Yes, they do rust inside in time, especially if they are not kept well filled. Stainless steel or fabric tanks will not rust but are quite rare.

How big should the tanks be? The larger they are, the less often you have to refuel. Apart from being more convenient, large tanks allow you to travel with less worry in areas (such as rural France, for example) where fueling points are widely separated. However, there is a trade off between space for tanks and that for accommodation. A 500-litre tank will allow you to cruise for about 100 hours between refuellings.

Diesel floats on water, so condensation inside the tank collects at the bottom. This should be removed once in a while, which requires a drain cock right at the bottom of the tank. There should also be cocks in the fuel lines to allow the fuel to be shut off for repairs or in an emergency. A remote shut-off outside the engine room, ideally accessible from the helm, is a good safety feature but often absent. Each tank needs a breather (an air pipe out of the top of the tank) which must vent outside the hull and should be above the level of the filler cap. A level indicator is handy, but transparent glass tubes are now outlawed in most countries and gauges or dip sticks are usual.

It is essential for the fuel to be filtered on its way from tank to engine. If the filtration is not good enough, you soon have expensive problems with the injectors or other equipment. Two types of filter are needed. First, a sedimenter or water trap – basically a sealed bowl with an inlet and outlet at the top. The bowl is removed occasionally to empty out any nasty stuff which has collected in it. Second, one or more fine filters. These are usually attached to the engine itself and take the form of replaceable cartridges. All filters should be easy to get at. Best practice is to have two fuel supply pipes, each with its own filters, so if one gets clogged (and stops the engine, as always happens at the most inconvenient time possible) you can immediately switch to the other while you replace the clogged filters. A common cause of clogging is rust washing off the inside of the fuel tanks during a passage through rough water.

Another type of fuel tank you may find is a day tank. This is a small tank mounted high up, and usually holds about a day's consumption of fuel. Typically it is connected to the main tank via a hand pump. Historically it was used as a further measure for filtering the diesel. Also, older engine types often required a gravity fuel feed, which meant a tank above the engine. Today we can do without day tanks since diesel is cleaner, filters are more effective and automatic fuel lifting pumps are almost universal. But they do no harm.

Diesel is inherently safe as it is quite hard to get it to burn or explode, but regulations are tightening up. We cannot tell you all the current rules but it is usually quite easy to comply with them by making relatively minor changes to the installed fuel system.

DRIVE

For the engine to move the barge, its power has to be converted into a push against the water. There are a number of elements making up the 'drive': the gearbox or transmission, the shaft and the propeller.

The functions of the transmission are to deliver the engine power to the shaft; to make the shaft rotate in forward, reverse, or not at all (neutral); and to make the shaft spin more slowly than the engine ('reduction'). Large slow-turning propellers are more efficient than smaller ones turning at engine speed.

The conventional approach is a marine gearbox bolted to a bell-shaped housing at the flywheel end of the engine. The gearbox power input shaft engages with a drive plate attached to the flywheel (where a clutch would be in a car). At the other end of the gearbox its output shaft is connected to the inboard end of the propeller shaft.

Marine gearboxes have to be very tough. They take all the shocks of going into forward and reverse (changes often made far too quickly), and those of the propeller hitting something solid. Often they incorporate the thrust bearing, which is the bit of the barge the propeller shaft pushes against to make the barge move (but if not there should be a stand-alone thrust bearing

somewhere along the propeller shaft). However, there comes a time when even the best gearbox cannot stand any more (ab)use, so any strange gearbox noises should definitely worry you. They are expensive (£1,000 plus) to repair or replace, although there are specialist reconditioners who sometimes offer good deals on exchange units.

A gearbox is not the only option. Power can be transmitted successfully by hydraulics, electricity, or even belts. However, all these are rare so we will not discuss them further here.

The propeller shaft will be supported on one or more bearings; it goes through the hull in a stern tube which has a device (a grease-filled gland, for example) for preventing water coming in. The stern tube bearing, typically a large brass bushing, will wear in time, particularly if it has been used in dirty water. Checking for this should be part of the survey.

Although the propeller is outside the engine room, it seems most sensible to deal with this item here. It is usually three- (occasionally four-) bladed, made of bronze or steel. Do not worry about which. It may be over 65 cm in diameter and be worth hundreds of pounds. Best if it is not too bent or chewed! Propeller sizes are specified in diameter x pitch (pitch is how far the propeller would theoretically screw forward through water in one revolution), and a replacement must have a hub big enough to accept the size of propeller shaft already installed.

The propeller must be matched properly to both the engine and drive if the engine is to work efficiently. This matching is rather a black art, but if the barge seems to go much too fast at the lowest engine speed, or if it does not reach a normal engine speed when cruising, there is probably a mismatch. Seek specialist advice if you suspect this to be the case.

Some propeller suppliers have computer programs which calculate the specifications of propeller needed. In most cases they will feed your data in free of charge in the hope of selling you a propeller. To save you a second call if you use this service, here is the information you will need to supply:

- Maximum engine revolutions/minute
- Engine power
- Drive reduction ratio
- Maximum diameter of the propeller you can accommodate
- Length and maximum beam at the waterline
- Draft (or, occasionally, displacement and maximum hull speed).

However, even with the services of a computer, the match may turn out to be not quite right, so adjust your expectations accordingly.

If there is a mismatch, correction may require installing a different propeller of the right size, the hub of which will probably need machining so that its mounting hole fits the shaft perfectly.

It is a feature of many barges that the stern moves sideways as well as backwards when the transmission is in reverse. This is called the 'paddle wheel effect', as it is caused by the propeller acting as a paddle wheel because the water pressure is lower at its top than its bottom. If the propeller is too near the surface of the water, it can cavitate (drawing in air instead of water), losing effectiveness and vibrating nastily. Both these effects can be reduced by anti-cavitation plates, metal strips or a tube near the propeller. Unfortunately, these can make it difficult for you to fish with a boat hook to clear the inevitable rubbish that propellers attract (nothing is all to the good).

Although it is quite easy to move the stern sideways with the engine, moving the bow can be another story, particularly when space is limited, there is a cross wind and there are crushable small craft nearby. One answer is the bow thruster, a small propeller mounted cross-wise in a tube near the bow. This may be driven hydraulically from the main engine, electrically, or directly by its own small diesel engine. However, there are drawbacks here too. Bow thrusters are usually used only in short bursts, which can mean their diesel engines never warm up and may wear unusually quickly. Their propellers can suck in rubbish, which can do a lot of damage in the confining tube. For some types, the engine and tube can take up a significant amount of space which could otherwise provide highly desirable storage area or part of a cabin. A bow thruster is a very useful tool but if the purchase price is boosted because of it, make sure it works properly. Many barges do not have one.

Anti-cavitation plates

2.4.2 NAVIGATION

STEERING

To cruise where you want to, you need to be able to point the barge in the right direction. Barges usually have large rudders to allow you to achieve this, but there are a few variations in how the rudder is moved.

Originally, barges (especially sailing barges) were steered by a tiller, a large wooden bar, often beautifully carved, attached to the top of the rudder. Many older barges still are steered this way. Tiller steering is very direct and quick and requires little maintenance but is not universally loved. It can require considerable strength, especially in rough weather. And the steerer almost always has to stand outside, rain or shine.

Many barges originally steered by tillers have been converted to wheel steering. The rest had this from the start. The traditional approach is a large wheel which pulls the rudder by means of chains (or cables) connected to a quadrant on the rudder shaft. Nowadays, it is good safety practice (and the law in some countries) that the wheel have an outer rim attached to the end of the spokes if it is the of 'ship's wheel' type. You really do not want to have your arm (or anything else) between the spokes if the rudder hits something hard or meets a large wave. Chain steering is perfectly all right but can be a little heavy if it takes only a few turns of the wheel to go from full starboard to full port. You do not want there to be too many turns, as this can slow you down seriously in emergency manoeuvring.

Another option is hydraulic steering, where a small hydraulic pump is attached to the wheel shaft and a ram to the rudder quadrant. This may require less space (and sometimes less maintenance) than a chain system. Some hydraulic steering is powered, thus reducing the size of steerer's biceps required. However, some powered hydraulic steering systems provide almost no feedback (feel as to what the rudder is doing), which can be disconcerting. Also, there is slightly more machinery which could break down. On the other hand, you can dispense with the wheel and replace it with a joystick if you wish!

NAVIGATION INSTRUMENTS

Some barges have no navigation instruments because they have never needed them on the quiet inland routes. But you may be going farther afield, so if your purchase comes with a fuller inventory it could save you money later.

If you ever expect to be travelling in the dark, fog or snow, you will need navigation lights. Lights of the proper size for a barge cost more than you might think (plus installation, of course), so it is a definite plus if a barge already has them. The full set is port (red), starboard (green), stern (white pointing backwards), bow (white pointing forward), and anchor (white all around). A spotlight and headlight (for tunnels) is also recommended.

All barges must have an effective horn. These vary from the portable and mouth-operated to large air trumpets with their own compressors.

It is difficult nowadays to get away without a VHF radio. Many ports insist that vessels communicate with them by VHF, and you can save a lot of time by calling ahead when approaching one of the many locks which are VHF-equipped. In mainland Europe each VHF radio must automatically identify itself (i.e. you) at the start of each call; many older models cannot do this.

If you are venturing on to larger waters, you may need a compass. This is by no means a universal fitting. Some barges (few, admittedly) have not only a compass but also global positioning equipment (GPS), radar and depth sounder.

Finally, have you wondered why our Association called its journal *Blue Flag*? A blue flag is a piece of equipment, peculiar to barges, which is essential if you use mainland Europe river navigations. A vessel coming upstream which wishes to pass 'on the wrong side' (i.e. starboard to starboard) to avoid heavy current can display a blue flag to indicate its intentions. Today this is no longer a flag but a tilting blue board with a flashing white light, usually mounted just outside the wheel house.

OTHER

You will not always stop alongside a canal bank. And there will not always be a mooring buoy. Sometimes you will have to anchor. Each barge should have a suitable anchor (at the bow), a significant length of heavy chain, and a winch to get the whole lot back on board. A powered winch is a bonus (if it works properly) but a manual one can do the job just fine, if slowly. Another (usually smaller) anchor at the stern can be very handy too, especially for stopping in a hurry when heading downstream.

Towing a dinghy can cause problems, particularly in locks, so you need to be able to get the dinghy on board (and have somewhere to stow it). Traditional Dutch dinghies are made of steel and weigh just as much as you imagine.

Even wooden dinghies can be hard to lift. A davit, a small crane for lifting dinghies, is a useful fitting (doubling up for hanging flower baskets).

2.4.3 SAFETY

Safety on the water is critical. You need to keep it in mind the entire time. Do not ever forget that a barge is a ship, not a floating apartment. A full discussion of safety does not belong in this

handbook, but the following items are worth checking when you view barges.

You may need to escape from the vessel in a hurry if it starts to sink or catches fire. Does every room on board have adequate exits?

If the vessel gets into rough weather, waves may come over the top of the hull. Will the barge shed this water quickly and completely? If there is a well deck or cockpit, is it adequately drained?

Most barges were originally designed with water-tight bulkheads creating three or more separate compartments (bow, hold and stern). This would ensure that the barge remained afloat even if one compartment filled with water as the result of swamping, collision or a leak. Conversion may have resulted in the piercing or removal of one or both bulkheads as they can limit interior layout flexibility and efficiency. This is not necessarily a problem, but you (and some insurers) may feel more comfortable if the bulkheads are still intact.

Any pipe can spring a leak, so every fitting which passes water through the hull under water must have a sea cock (shut off valve) immediately inside the hull. Check for these, as the safety inspectors certainly will, and check that they work. Older or amateur conversions may have omitted them.

Finally, in case water does start getting in, there must be ways of getting it out again. Bilge pumps vary in sophistication, from hand-operated to fully automatic electric. There should be at least one in every watertight compartment, with a mix of electrical and mechanical (manual or directly driven by the engine) in case of electricity failure. Electric pumps with water-sensing switches are worthwhile, particularly if you leave the barge unattended for longer periods. You do not want to come back and find it has sunk as the result of a small leak!

2.5 THE CONVERSION

Conversion makes a former freight-carrying barge suitable for cruising and living on.

You may decide to convert your barge yourself (using your own hands or with the help of a boat builder or yard). However, fewer and fewer barges are available straight out of trade so you may have to remove an existing conversion and start again. This is quite feasible, and might be the only way to get the layout you want. It also allows you to stipulate the materials and quality of workmanship and to install new equipment. However, a substantial re-conversion may be much more expensive than retaining the existing conversion and making only minor alterations, so beware.

We should issue a general warning here. Work on barges always takes much longer and costs much more than you initially estimate – and unreasonably more than equivalent work on land-based homes or equipment.

After those gloomy thoughts, we move on to the more uplifting questions of what you might want and look for in a conversion.

We assume you have by now made the decisions as to what you want from the ship and where your main cruising ground will be. This is your basis for judging the conversion. Before you settle on what you actually need, answer questions such as:

- How many berths do you really need? (Cruising with large numbers on board can become somewhat tiring after a while)
- Must berths be in private bedrooms, or will dormitory-style bunks do?
- Will you use the ship primarily for cruising, or mainly as a static residence with occasional trips?
- Who will use the ship? How robust are they?
- Will you be on board in winter?
- What type of interior do you prefer (traditional, modern, light, dark, types of furnishing and fabrics)?
- What household equipment do you consider essential, and what would you prefer in an ideal world?

Try to look at as many interiors as possible. No two barges or conversions are the same. The more you see, the more interesting ideas you will come across. Most barge owners are only too happy to talk about and show off their vessels, and boat shows often have larger craft on display.

Do not forget that although hull, engine, navigation equipment etc. are all vital to any boat owner, if the ship fails to provide somewhere warm, dry, and inviting, with the potential for a hot meal after a long day's cruising, you probably will not be happy with it.

What follows is a brief description of the main elements of a conversion. Conversion merits a book of its own, so we have limited ourselves to hitting the high points – suggesting the principal choices you may come across and giving some basic ideas on good practice.

2.5.1 STARTING FROM THE OUTSIDE

The overall shape of the conversion governs what you can put in it and whether the barge looks right. An attractively shaped hull can be ruined by a clumsy cabin top. There are a lot of the latter, and they can be expensive to reshape. However, it is a matter of taste whether the top of the conversion is flat or follows the sheer (curve) of the hull. Either can look good.

Size of the conversion can vary considerably for a given hull. Some use virtually the entire length of the craft, maximising floor space while leaving just enough room outside to navigate the vessel (there really *must* be enough for safe working); others have spacious open decks for socialising in warm climes. Some have full-standing height throughout, others may have (for example) lower fore-cabins. Most are built on the original coamings (the raised metal edges around the hold which the hatch covers sit on), but some have achieved more interior room by narrowing the side decks.

Some ships have a wheelhouse which, in effect, adds another room and makes for pleasantly sociable cruising (but you lose its use when it is demounted). Others have a basic box with just enough room inside for the steerer. In mainland Europe, many wheelhouses are fixed, which can be a problem with the lower bridges found in the UK. Most wooden wheelhouses can be made demountable, but steel ones usually cannot and may need replacing in wood. This is not cheap, particularly if you use traditional teak.

Many conversions retain an original stern cabin behind a full-width engine room, with the bulk of the accommodation in the former hold, but this is by no means the only possibility. Although the original cabin can provide a completely separate room (or even a small suite), useful for privacy if you plan to run the barge on charter or want to get away from your guests when cruising, you may have to climb

awkwardly through the wheelhouse to get to it. Not handy if the wheelhouse is demounted and it is raining.

Some types of barge allow for a passage past the engine room, linking bow and stern accommodation on one level. Others now have the engine right at the stern, consolidating all the accommodation forward. On most barges the main entrance is via the wheelhouse. But not always; some welcome you at the bow.

A brief note on the material used in the conversion shell: the large majority are in steel, which provides flexibility of alteration and ease of maintenance and repair. Some wooden ones are found, but extra caution is needed to avoid rot and (often very hard to cure) roof leaks.

Think about windows. Beware the greenhouse look. You may want some wall space for pictures and cupboards. Seaworthy windows are well worth having, double-glazed and with heat-insulated frames if possible: these help avoid the potentially serious problem of condensation running off the glass in cooler weather and subsequent lining rot. Note whether the windows can be left ajar in the rain without getting your carpets wet (preferably not opening outwards, as this makes them very vulnerable to contact with waterway structures and other craft). Can they be securely locked shut if you go on open water or leave the craft unoccupied?

2.5.2 SYSTEMS

A barge needs all the systems of a house, and more. They tend to be more complex than domestic ones because they must usually be able to operate (at least for a while) independently of the municipal utilities. Beware, though. Some barges which have been converted for strictly residential use actually do depend on shore hook-ups, and may have no independent systems at all. When they untie from the bank, the power goes off, the taps run dry and the phone goes dead!

WATER

Barge domestic water systems have several main components:

- One or more tanks
- One or more pressure pumps
- A method of heating water
- Distribution piping and fixtures.

Tanks are made from a range of materials. The best is probably stainless steel, but polypropylene (rigid plastic), plastic fabric (in a supporting box), and fibreglass are all acceptable. They must be leak-proof and have proper support (a full tank is heavy, and you do not want it to move if the barge rolls). They also should be symmetrical across the barge (so no list develops when water gets low), and accessible for cleaning and repairs. Larger ones need internal baffles to stop the contents surging about. Be sure to check that they are not growing green crops inside (although these can be cleared up).

The total water storage volume you need depends on how much water you will use (how many people, bath or shower, summer or winter, etc.) and how long you will be forced to go between fills. Also, on how much of the barge's internal space you want to sacrifice to tankage (this applies to storing waste and fuel as well as water).

Most water systems are pressurised, usually by an automatic electric pump with a pressure switch (although hand-pumping can still be found). The more expensive the pump, the higher the flow. Water pump noise can be intrusive, particularly at night, so pumps shuld be carefully located and sound-insulated.

Water heating is usually by an on-demand gas burner or a hot water tank. The tank can be heated by a calorifier coil using waste heat from the main engine or from a water-cooled generator (a very worthwhile arrangement for saving fuel), a (separate) calorifier coil from the central heating system, an electric element (if there is a connection to shore power, or a large generator), or a combination of these.

Piping is usually copper, or more recently plastic. DIY piping systems are common but workmanship varies widely. Convenient valves at low points for draining the system, and bleeders at high points for removing air, are important. Insulation of the pipes is advisable.

WASTE WATER REMOVAL

Waste water from barges is of two types: grey water (from sinks and baths) and sewage (from toilets).

In most places it is legal to discharge grey water straight into whatever you are floating in. There are a couple of points to consider. Are the drains above or below the waterline? Above is slightly safer, below avoids negative comments from passers-by. Are the fixtures (particularly the bath or shower) above water level or do they require a drain pump? Drain pumps on baths and showers are prone to corrosion and clogging with hair, so can have quite short lives unless fitted with effective hair traps.

The traditional Dutch solution to sewage disposal was to mount the toilet on a large vertical pipe opening out through the bottom of the barge. Use of these, and other 'sea toilets', is illegal in most UK inland waters and probably soon will be in other European countries. The approved answer is some form of holding tank which is emptied into shore sewer facilities.

Holding tanks are made of the same range of materials as water tanks, but the preference for stainless steel may be stronger here due to the rather more unpleasant consequences of leakage. Size of tank will again depend on the usage of the craft, and whether you use water-flush toilets. Other toilets vary from simple drop-through ones which mount on top of the tank (in the simplest case the tank is portable and carried to the disposal point) to macer-ator-pump equipped conventional house toilets, to high-tech vacuum systems which minimise flushing water (sometimes canal water is drawn in by a separate pump for flush toilets).

Shore disposal facilities often include tank pump-out services at a fee, but you may wish to have your own pump to avoid these charges and for added flexibility. These need to be robust, quite high volume, and able to deal with water with a high solid content. With the right plumbing, they can double as emergency bilge pumps, bath draining pumps or for running a deck hose.

Other rarer options include chemical toilets and electrically powered biosystems which freeze-dry the waste down to granule form.

ELECTRICITY

Most barges have a DC electrical system, like a car or caravan. Some are 12 volt, but many are 24 volt. The latter system results in lower current for the same power and so can be built with wiring of smaller cross-section, but 24 volt equipment is slightly less readily available (but many larger trucks use 24 volt, so it is not really a problem).

Such a system has a battery set. The capacity of this is measured in amp-hours or kilowatt-hours, but you should not expect to make effective use of more than about half the stated capacity due to the physics of the ubiquitous lead-acid battery. Batteries more than five years old are suspect, and they are not cheap to replace. Check that there is a separate battery for starting the engine, as you would not want to be rendered immobile because someone ran down the domestic battery by falling asleep in front of the late movie on TV.

Batteries have to be recharged. The barge should have one or more means of doing this. The simplest is an alternator on the propulsion engine. This is not a good total solution if the barge is likely to remain stationary, as long periods of running a large diesel with only the alternator for a load will shorten the engine's life significantly.

A better option is to have a mains-powered charger too (for when the barge is not moving). This requires a mooring with mains laid on, of course. Such a charger need not be large as it can conveniently be left running for long periods.

The best solution is an on-board generator, preferably diesel, coupled to a larger charger. Petrol is legal on barges but not recommended due to its safety problems.

Generator engines can be either air- or water-cooled. Air-cooled ones may be cheaper but are noisier, an important consideration to both you and your neighbours when you remember how long generators have to run. Also, you cannot use the waste heat from an air-cooled engine to warm your water, but instead have to vent the hot air to the outside.

With a generator, a more potent charger is merited to reduce recharging (and thus generator running) time. For 24 volt systems, 50 amps is a common rating, but 75 or even 100 amps are also found. Charger technology varies considerably and is evolving rapidly, and an older machine may not recharge a battery nearly as quickly as a new one with the same amperage rating.

Since the generator will almost always be 240 volts AC, it can not only power a charger but also provides mains current to (a separate system of) wiring through the barge. This will enable you to use all your usual domestic equipment and appliances, which will be much cheaper than equivalent DC versions.

A charger requires 2kVa to 3kVa, and a washing machine or dishwasher 3kVa. So if you expect to use the normal range of domestic electrical equipment, you should look for a generator in the 6kVa to 10kVa range. Anything larger will probably be too lightly loaded for its own good, and waste space.

The 240V system will only be of use when the barge is plugged into the shore or the generator is running. Unless, that is, there is an inverter, a device which changes battery power to house power. Many barges now have these. They have a smaller output than a mid-sized generator (usually under 3kW) but make life pleasanter when cruising. Good large-output inverters are not cheap, but it may be possible to recoup their costs by the savings made by using 240V equipment. Several reputable brands are available, with Victron and Mastervolt probably at the forefront at present.

Without meaning to drag you into technicalities, we should point out that there is AC – and AC. Certain inverters produce electricity that some appliances (particularly electronic ones) do not like. 'Square wave' is not as good as 'modified sine wave'. Plain 'sine wave' is best but rarely found (and, as is the way of the world, requires the most expensive equipment to produce).

More modern barge electrical systems often include one more piece of equipment which you may not have heard of: the isolation transformer. This is located between the electrical connection to the shore and the barge's on-board 240 volt wiring. Its purpose is to prevent stray electrical currents which can all too easily flow back to ground through the barge's hull and the water when you are plugged in to the mains, and which can in the worst cases cause the hull to corrode with quite frightening speed. One can always be added later, but they cost several hundred pounds. If there is not one, and the barge has been much on the mains, pay particular attention to the hull thicknesses on the survey report (*discussed later*).

Wiring systems merit close inspection. Many have been installed or altered by amateurs and can be death traps. A tidy installation, with well supported cabling clear of the bilges and with adequate circuit breakers, is the minimum to look for unless you are prepared for a lot of remedial work. The wire itself should preferably be multi-strand as opposed to single-core, as the latter can become brittle at terminals and snap over time due to vibration (safety regulations are beginning to make multi-strand a requirement).

Think about where and what electricity outlets you require, as it is not easy to add additional cables to a fully lined-out craft. Remember to consider the range of lighting you will need.

HEATING AND VENTILATION

There are as many types of heating system as there are preferences, from solid fuel stoves to sophisticated programmable diesel furnaces or boilers.

Solid fuel needs storage with easy loading access for the bulky coal or wood. Many people would not be without the cheerfulness of a real fire, and a lot of barges have them. But remember the drawbacks of ash and dust..... One way of having your cake *and* (h)eating it is a hearth-effect diesel or gas burner.

Gas equipment (for space or water heating) is compact and needs little maintenance. However, bottled gas (propane is better, because butane loses pressure in cold weather) is a much more expensive fuel than oil per unit of heat. Also, because it is more bulky, you have to keep changing those cumbersome bottles, and there are different types of bottles in different countries. Some safety authorities are starting to look unfavourably at some on-demand gas water heaters.

Diesel-burning hot-air or hot-water systems are increasingly popular. Many barges benefit from a constantly-burning heat source in cold weather. But for summer and autumn, the extra flexibility of a fire-on-demand programmable system, such as those made by Wesbasto and Eberspacher, is a bonus. They are more complex and require correspondingly more maintenance, and create a constant electrical drain.

As in a house, a comfortable barge should have a heat source in each room, including the wheelhouse. Make sure there are, or is room for, enough radiators and, especially in larger vessels, a suitable hot water circulating pump.

Ventilation is important. Fresh air is needed for breathing. Less obvious is the fact that people and domestic activities produce a lot of moisture which must be eliminated. Failure to do this will not only fog your windows, it will cause water to condense behind the cabin linings, leading to serious rot and other damage. Sufficient fixed vents at  both high and low levels should be fitted in addition to windows (which you will want to keep closed in bad weather). This is now a requirement in Great Britain. Bilges also need ventilating to avoid rot in the floors.

2.5.3 LINING

INSULATION

In the summer you will want your ship to stay cool inside; in winter you will want it to retain as much heat as possible. So insulation is a major consideration. It should be one of the first, too. It is often difficult to install or upgrade insulation after the interior finish is done.

Special fire-proof foam insulation sprayed on to clean dry steel work is easily the best way to insulate the top and sides. It must be applied professionally. Fibreglass or rock wool, battened to but slightly clear of the steel work and covered with a sealed heavy duty PVC moisture barrier, are traditional. Whereas foam 5cm thick gives good insulation, fibreglass needs to be 7.5 or 10cm thick.

Every gap between the steel and internal linings should be filled with insulation, and sealed with a moisture barrier. Check carefully that this is the case, as otherwise you will get cold spots and (worse still) condensation in the walls no matter how well you ventilate.

Be careful to check that combustible material is not applied directly against the hull. This would be dangerous if you needed some repair welding.

WALLS

Traditionally, lining is made of plywood, water-resistant if not full marine quality. Waterproof MDF (medium density fibreboard) is also acceptable.

Better interior walls are a sandwich of two linings with the space between filled with insulation. They improve sound privacy and add a measure of fire retardance. Solid doors give a better feeling of quality than those in plywood.

Ceilings can vary from wood planking to painted MDF. Walls can be finished in almost anything from paint to carpet.

The real decision for you, the purchaser, is whether you can stand the former owner's layout and taste and the quality of the work, or whether you will have to do minor or extensive refitting/redecorating. Yet again, this sort of work always seems to cost that much more than it does in land accommodation.

FLOORS

Varnished planks, cork, and vinyl are easy care, but carpets can be vacuumed rather than swept or polished and are warmer in winter. Dutch families who used to work the barges insisted that outdoor shoes be removed before entering the living accommodation. After you have tracked large sections of towpath on to your nice pale rugs you may want to adopt this rule too.

However, one consideration the first-time buyer often overlooks (and this applies to exterior walls below the water line) is that you may need access to the hull from the inside for repairs. A floor covered with carpet tiles can be easier to take up than one with wall-to-wall. Loose-lay vinyl is preferable to the glued-down variety. Smaller supporting or backing panels screwed into place allow quicker and easier access than do large sheets nailed down. Check how awkward it would be to take apart the interior structure in time of need.

BALLAST

Perhaps this is not really a conversion item, but the topic fits here.

Barges were designed to carry heavy weights, so they float high in the water when converted for leisure: sometimes too high, overall or at one end, for good manoeuvring or for getting under bridges. The solution is ballast, high density material usually installed under the floors.

Ideally, ballast should be removable so that the trim of the barge can be adjusted if need be and so that you can get at the inside of the hull. Removable ballast might comprise pieces of iron, bricks, concrete blocks etc.. In contrast, some barges are ballasted with concrete cast in place. This can be removed only by a jackhammer, a very tedious job. It has advantages in terms of strengthening the hull and protecting the interior from corrosion, but the French authorities disapprove of it because it is so hard to get out when a sunken vessel needs to be raised. Overall, this type of ballast must now be considered negatively.

Best practice demands a small air space between the ballast and the hull, to allow ventilation and drainage and to prevent the ballast moving and damaging the hull plating.

FURNITURE

The vendor may not leave you much portable furniture, but there may be quite a bit built in. Are there enough cupboards and drawers of a suitable shape? Are the beds long enough, and spaces above the mattress high enough for normal people (people in the past were not as tall as nowadays)?

If you have some beloved furniture you intend to install, do not forget to check whether you can get it on board. Barge doorways are seldom of standard domestic size. But maybe there is a large and removable skylight or hatch?

For any soft furniture, check that the foam or other filling meets current fire-retardance standards. Much does not, and these regulations are being enforced ever more toughly.

Too much free-standing furniture may not be a good idea. It can move alarmingly when the barge is in rough water.

OTHER

Varnished woodwork can be beautiful (although too much can make the world seem awfully brown). If it needs revarnishing, there might be a lot of work ahead. If the varnish has deteriorated near windows, the essential anti-ultra-violet type which resists the effects of sunlight may not have been used. Many people now opt for modern woodstain preservative treatments, especially for external wood work. It does not have the same high gloss but is much more user-friendly.

2.5.4 DOMESTIC EQUIPMENT

Any gadgets you have in your house, you can have in your barge.

Let us start with the kitchen (or galley).

The overwhelming choice for barge cookers is bottled propane, because gas burners are instantly adjustable. Unfortunately propane is heavier than air and, if the system leaks, can collect very dangerously in the bilge. If there is any gas system on board, look for electronic gas-detectors. You also find oil or solid fuel occasionally (Aga-type stoves are sometimes installed, but beware! They can cook you as well as your food in summer). Electric cooking is possible but usually requires a generator to be kept running.

Lots of equipment can be installed in a well planned galley

Barge fridges can also be gas, but increasingly are electric. 'Yachty' DC fridges are much more expensive than the conventional domestic AC fridges. Toasters, mixers, etc.? Almost exclusively AC, so now you see why inverters are ever more popular. Although a 2kW inverter can readily handle a fridge (given enough battery capacity), a dishwasher, washer, or dryer will need 3kW or more, and may better be run off a generator.

3 COSTS OF OWNERSHIP

Even if you never leave the mooring, the cost of barge ownership definitely does not end with the purchase cheque. Barges can certainly be a cheap way to live, but do not underestimate costs such as moorings, licensing, regular docking and so on which defray the more obvious savings.

The mistake some buyers make is to overlook important ongoing expenses. We bring the main running costs to your attention below, to help you avoid getting in over your head (figuratively, of course).

3.1 NAVIGATION CHARGES

Inland navigations and harbours are governed by navigation authorities which levy a (usually) annual charge for keeping or using a craft on their waters. These charges vary substantially from authority to authority, both in their magnitude and in how they are calculated.

Even the Environment Agency (EA), which manages navigation on a few UK rivers, does not have a uniform approach. On the non-tidal Thames, its charges vary with the length x beam of the craft. This number is multiplied by a standard charge/m^2/ year, currently (1998) £8.38. So the owner of a 20m x 4m barge could be stuck with a bill of £670 per year. However, on the non-tidal Medway, another EA river, the calculation is based only on length, and capped at 11m. The same craft would attract a charge of only £141 a year if kept there.

The British Waterways Board (BWB), which controls most other UK river navigations and most canals, makes charges according to length, setting different rates depending on whether you want to use the rivers only, or the whole system. To use the River Lee navigation, for example, the BWB might charge £200 per year. To use the same barge on the canals as well, the fee would be about £400 per year.

To make things even more complex, EA charges for a 'houseboat' are about half those for a cruiser, but it defines a houseboat as one with no means of propulsion. On the other hand, BWB charges for houseboats have been about double those for cruisers, and on these waters 'houseboats' are allowed engines!

Each smaller navigation and harbour authority has its own charging scheme.

A final thought on navigation charges. If you venture off your home waters into those of another navigation authority, the other authority will require you to pay its charges for the time you are there, usually at a higher daily rate than you pay (pro-rated from annual charges) at home. You will not get a rebate from your home authority for time you are away.

The French require each vessel to have a vignette, which can be bought for varying periods and for which the charge is based on length x beam. The French cap their charges at 60m^2. Dutch waterways still tend to be free; Belgium makes a relatively nominal charge.

3.2 INSURANCE

All barges must be insured. This is not only for your peace of mind; more and more navigation authorities insist on seeing proof of your insurance before they will let you on to their waters.

You will probably want three types of insurance cover: hull, third party liability, and contents.

3.2.1 HULL AND THIRD PARTY LIABILITY

It might be expected that insurance for big iron craft over 70 years old would be difficult and expensive to get. And so it was, but things have improved somewhat of late.

The major problem was the unfamiliarity of UK insurers with the risks involved. This led to over-caution, and high premiums. However, one of the founders of the Association managed to arrange a scheme particularly for barges a few years ago, and since then several other insurers have developed competing schemes. There is now a reasonable market.

Of course, Belgian and Dutch insurers knew all along that barges are reasonable insurance risks, being familiar with them and accustomed to vessels built in the 1890s still being in trade. Competitive premiums can be arranged for vessels based in the Netherlands. The obvious snag is the language problem. Policies are written in Dutch and governed by Dutch law. There is clearly a risk of misunderstandings, and potential difficulties in pursuing anything other than a straightforward claim.

Typical cover is for loss or damage to hull and major equipment, and against third party claims of up to £1,000,000 or more. The insured value is usually based on the purchase price or a professional valuation.

As a guide, with an excess (deductible from each claim) of £500, the annual premium for craft in UK inland waters (e.g. not below the Thames barrier) might be 1% of insured value, although there are signs that this rate may be dropping.

3.2.2 CONTENTS

Particularly if you will be living aboard, you will probably want insurance for your barge's contents. The cover for cruising, or for the residential use of the barge, is similar to the comprehensive insurance available to a householder, but also includes the risk of sinking. Extensions are available for personal possessions against all risks while you are away from your vessel. A typical annual premium is about 1% of the value of the contents insured.

3.3 MOORING

Although your mind will be focused on finding the barge, we should warn you that finding a satisfactory mooring, especially if you want to live on it in Britain, may prove to be a problem. In fact, moorings deserve a publication all to themselves, so although that is somewhat beyond the scope of this handbook do not think it does not deserve your attention.

The standard advice is 'Find your mooring before buying your barge' and we endorse this fully. However, it is fair to say that only a very small percentage of barge buyers follow this counsel.

In general, the situation is somewhat easier in other European countries than in Britain. Inexpensive short-term moorings can often be found in France, Belgium or the Netherlands but seldom in major cities even there. Amenable permanent moorings can usually be found with some research, but usually at a higher price.

The trouble is that barges are somewhat larger than your average cruiser, so most moorings are not designed to cater for them. Some marinas welcome barges, others will be horrified.

An important point to note is that there is a very significant difference between a mooring for a vessel used principally for cruising and one for a residential craft. Setting up a new residential mooring is subject to local government approval, which is not easily obtained in most cases. Boats on approved residential moorings often sell for much higher prices than the worth of the boat just because of the mooring, even though the mooring may have no security of tenure. It is not uncommon for someone to buy a boat he does not want, just to get its mooring. However, if thinking of this, check that putting a different craft on the mooring is allowed. Surprisingly often it is not.

Your broker (if you buy through one) may be a good place to start looking for a mooring, but do not be too optimistic.

Your hunt for a mooring must concentrate on the local area in which you wish to keep your ship. Do a bit of towpath walking, visit other boat owners, and you will probably get direct information on what is or is not available.

Moorings may be available from the navigation authority for the waterway concerned, from commercial mooring operators (marinas, inland ports, etc.), private riparian owners, and the secondary market (those who no longer need their moorings and wish to pass them on).

The EA does not operate moorings itself. Most river moorings are privately owned or managed. The EA does, however, possess and exercise a considerable degree of control over where moorings can be established, and what they can be used for. Do not assume that the purchase of freehold riverbank implies an automatic mooring right. If you are considering a mooring on EA waters, verify carefully with the appropriate EA office that a mooring there is acceptable.

BWB does administer some of the moorings on its system, but the majority are for non-residential craft only. For many years BWB had a policy of severely restricting residential moorings. Usually these were only available on a caretaker basis at boatyards. As a result, there developed a large number of 'permanently cruising' craft, some of which in fact did not cruise at all. As a consequence, the chances of a newcomer finding an approved residential mooring were very slim in many BWB areas. However, the Board has recently been changing its policies, and now cares much less what you do on your moored boat. The situation is not easy, but is somewhat better than it was.

There are many private moorings on both EA and BWB waters, from large basins to small lengths of bank. A few are residential, most strictly not, but some are in the grey area of unofficially residential. With these last you run the risk of suddenly finding that you may not live there any more as the result of some local government crackdown.

The Port of London Authority (PLA) controls mooring on the tidal Thames (i.e. below Teddington in west London) and operates some pier and buoy moorings itself. Possibilities have been very limited on the tideway to date, but more recently a number of new sites have opened and more possibilities are in the pipeline. There are some established marinas, many in former commercial docks such as South Dock, St. Katherine's and Chelsea Harbour, which accommodate barges, but these can be very expensive. Thistleworth Marine at Isleworth is an example of another approach, a moorings co-operative. However, the PLA has recently been reviewing its mooring licence charges (i.e. trying to raise them very substantially), so beware.

The tidal Medway and Swale estuaries in Kent are rich in possibilities, with marinas such as those at Hoo and Medway Bridge Marina offering berths, and possibilities in numerous creeks and corners. In almost every case these moorings will be drying, which means that your barge will sit on the mud, sometimes for most of the day, when the tide goes out. And since they are tidal, you will be floating in salt water which is less kind to metal craft than is fresh.

The further from London, the easier mooring becomes. You do not have be located in the Thames watershed.

Moorings are generally priced by length. As a guide, London Dockland moorings may go for £150/m/year, while a rural canal mooring well away from London might be only one third of that. (Please remember that this is in addition to any navigation charges.)

However, those charges may not be the whole story. You still have to consider utilities. Some moorings come with mains electricity and water, rubbish removal, the ability to hook up a phone, parking and perhaps even a sewer connection, and include these in the price. Others may not have these services available at all; still others expect you to make your own arrangements and pay for each separately, and some may act as middleman and take a mark-up.

In general, utilities will cost you as much or more than they do for a house. If you generate your own electricity, it will certainly cost you more per kilowatt-hour than the local electricity company charges. The purchase price of your generator takes the place of the standing charge. You may find a mobile telephone is the only sensible communications solution. Some now have free local calls but on average they still cost more than a fixed line (but connection charges are lower). If you heat with oil, you may end up ahead of the game, as your fuel will cost the same but barges are usually well insulated.

Finally, do not overlook local taxes. A barge is not real estate, but a mooring may be, and in the UK the local council tax (perhaps £400 per year or more) can apply to residential moorings.

3.4 MAINTENANCE

Like houses and cars, barges need regular maintenance. It certainly is not something to skimp on (not only will value decline, but it is much cheaper to keep a barge in good condition than it is to rehabilitate it later). And, of course, you do not want your barge to sink, even at its moorings.

The hull is most critical. This and underwater machinery, propeller, rudder, etc. are serviced when the barge is out of the water, in a dry dock or on a slipway or tidal grid. This must occur at least every six years (more frequently in some circumstances) which, apart from anything else, is a usual requirement of your hull insurer.

Docking can cost £100 to £200 per day, and you may need a week or more. While in dock, you will need a hull thickness survey (*see the section on surveys later on*) which may reveal some thin spots (anything less than 4mm) over which new plating must be welded. You may also want the hull pressure-washed to get rid of growth, or perhaps even sand-blasted and repainted if corrosion

1974 Gardner engine in a new installation

is setting in, but be careful of blasting riveted hulls as it can undesirably loosen things up. And while thinking of corrosion, you will likely need to replace the anodes, pieces of 'less noble' metal attached to the hull which, while corroding away themselves, prevent the hull from doing so.

Overall, a docking bill may reach thousands of pounds. And no, you cannot put it off safely for very long.

Docking a barge in the Netherlands and Belgium is usually cheaper, and the required work tends to be done more cheaply and more efficiently than in Britain because they have more yards, there is more competition and they are used to dealing with larger craft.

The barge's topsides need regular attention too. A good exterior cleaning every month or so is a start. If you have the electricity supply to run it, a pressure washer can be a good investment. Not only does this make the barge appear well cared for, but it also prevents grime standing on the paint and becoming a permanent stain. Repainting may be needed every four or five years, and varnished exterior woodwork needs redoing every two or three years.

Barring breakdowns, propulsion machinery and the generator should need only normal preventive maintenance (oil and filter changes etc.). New batteries should be budgeted for about every five years.

Domestic equipment and interior finishes require much the same attention as those in a house.

This section was not meant to scare you, but we do hope it has got rid of any impression that owning, or living on, a barge is a no-cost experience. However, as a small ray of hope, there are ways to reduce some costs, for example by sharing certain services or patronising suppliers known for competitive prices or discounts to DBA members. Information appears regularly in our magazine *Blue Flag*.

4 THE MARKET

You are unlikely to buy a barge immediately usable for cruising or residence for less than £30,000, and that would probably be a small one. At that price, you would probably need to begin by spending more money on repairs or missing amenities. On the other hand, you *could* spend up to £300,000 buying and converting a 30m barge to a reasonable standard. In general terms, £70,000 purchases a nice ship about 20m long, and £100,000 a very nice one (in 1997 prices).

The £100,000 barge might feel a better bargain than the £30,000 one, given all the equipment etc. that it comes with, which illustrates the point that it can be hard to get your money back if you do a luxury conversion.

Barges 17m–24m long by 3.5m–4.2m wide tend to attract premium prices. They have a wide cruising range, are of a manageable size to maintain and handle, and fit many moorings and docks.

Barges in the UK tend to sell for more than they do in the Netherlands, but that is often to take into account the cost of getting the barge there. Also, many conversions in mainland Europe are of substantially lower quality than those in the UK, and the UK has more stringent and compulsory safety rules and standards for equipment and installation.

The selection is usually better in the Netherlands. If you are looking for an unconverted barge, the Netherlands is probably the best place to start. However, the few small barges (i.e. shorter than 30m) still in trade are mostly used for bunkering tankers or as crane ships, with a lot of equipment (tanks, etc.) which has to be removed before conversion can start. Most smaller barges on the market are conversions. If you *can* find one, a vessel still in trade can be a good buy. It will probably have had to be kept in good condition to do its work. But be cautious about the reason for sale, as the barge may have reached the point where keeping it in working trim is no longer economic.

Older conversions, particularly those used as houseboats, deserve careful scrutiny. Hull maintenance may have been skimped, and the conversion may not come up current standards, especially with respect to gas and electricity systems. If they have been connected to the municipal utilities, their systems may not operate at all if they cast off.

5 THE SEARCH

5.1 WHERE TO LOOK

In the UK, barges for sale are advertised, either by owners or brokers, in various publications. *Boats & Planes for Sale* (a monthly advertising paper which contains craft for sale throughout Europe) can be fruitful. *Waterways World* (a monthly inland waterways magazine) has a few, but they will be annoyingly hidden among the narrow boat advertisements. The daily free-ads paper *Loot* sometimes turns up a few, usually under 'Houseboats'.

In France, barges appear for sale in *Fluvial,* a bi-monthly French equivalent of *Waterways World.*

In the Netherlands, *Schuttevaer,* a paper for the commercial barge trade, appears weekly. Although it is in Dutch, it will not take you long to pick up the key jargon, but it is mostly concerned with larger vessels still carrying freight. *Jacht & Bootgids* is a handy used-boat publication. Fortunately, most Dutch (a much higher proportion than the French) can carry out at least a limited conversation in English on the telephone.

Your new barge may not look like much when you first see it

5.2 BROKERS

Many barge purchases involve brokers. There are a number of good ones and they can be very good value for money.

In Britain, a broker normally works for and is responsible to the vendor, not to you the purchaser. In the Netherlands, things can be different and a broker will happily work for the purchaser to find a suitable vessel (although unless you have agreed otherwise, he will be working for the vendor). He will either claim a finding commission if you buy something he has found for you, or charge a fee in advance for a number of introductions. Practices vary, but it would be reasonable in negotiating any brokerage charges in advance to establish whether the broker is also being paid by the vendor.

Dutch brokers may advertise barges, and be able to source barges from other brokers. Dutch practice is that potential buyers deal with one broker only, who will if necessary offer barges from other brokers, sharing their commission by agreement. If you contact a number of brokers and they find they are all separately looking for the same barge for the same client, they will not be happy.

Brokers are less common in France, and in fact barge sales there are often more like those of houses and often do not involve a survey (as a result of stringent French laws on misrepresentation). However, these may not be much comfort to you when you are in another country, so insist on a survey even in France.

Not all brokers have the same idea of what constitutes appropriate business ethics. Before you sign up with one, ask around. Other barge owners are often very willing to talk about good, bad and legendary experiences with individual brokers.

6 VIEWING

So you are still eager to be a barge owner. You are itching to go and look at some craft. But what will you look out for?

This section is to help you with the first kick-the-tyres inspection (fenders, that is, although the French frown on using tyres for this) which you may be doing on your own, and which should enable you to weed out obvious duds early on.

6.1 INSPECTING A BARGE

We suggest you go through something like the following examination. We have listed the crucial things first, so you can soon stop wasting time on a clearly unsuitable vessel.

Always take notes. Photos too, if possible. Apart from the need to remember anything which worries you or which you want to question, you will find that the barges you see will tend to run together in your mind if you do not keep a record of each. You do not need to try to memorise this section before you head for the boatyard: just photocopy the check list in the Appendix.

6.1.1 HULL AND TOP

The first thing to check is whether the ship as a whole is any use to you. Is it a type you would be happy with? Does it (or can it be made to) sail, if that is what you want? Is it the right size (do not take the owner's word for this, but get out your tape measure)?

We assume you want a craft that is basically sound and will not need too much remedial work. Stand back and take a look at the hull. Is it straight? If it is significantly dented or knocked about, this may indicate a hard working life, but it could merely be evidence of a previous owner with weak steering skills. Apart from aesthetics, dents and knocks can be a problem because they may have provided locations for corrosion to start. Failure to have had dents repaired may also indicate a less-than-caring attitude on the part of a previous owner; this may show up in slackness elsewhere in the vessel. Can you see signs of pitting or corrosion along the water line, which may indicate extensive overplating will be needed?

What does the conversion look like? Is it aesthetic, or clumsy? Does it make good use of the hull, or is it wasteful? Can you get around outside easily when on board, and have you room to tend ropes etc.?

What is the top made of? Does it have any obvious flaws (look particularly closely if it is wooden)? What types of window does it have?

Have a look at the inside of the plating. There should be ways of doing this, perhaps by unscrewing wall or floor panels. Do you see rust? Not good, unless it is very minor. The inside of the hull should be protected from rusting with paint and, preferably, a coating of special grease. The space between the lining and the hull will often be moist, no place to allow rust to establish a hold.

Last, is there water in the bilge? Most barges leak a little through the stern gland, so a small amount of water inside is not necessarily a sign of trouble. However, if there are signs that there has been a lot recently, or if an automatic bilge pump comes on while you are on board (particularly if it comes on twice!), you probably should be concerned about how the water is getting in. While down there, check the type of ballast, and how it has been installed.

6.1.2 INTERIOR

What is the first general impression of the interior? Is it clean and well maintained, or scruffy? If the latter, is it just dirt, or long-term neglect which will be expensive to remedy? Remember, bringing a barge back into condition can involve a great deal of work, and you may not want to tackle redoing all the interior finishes.

Take a sniff. Can you smell damp, or worse, mildew? If so, find its source. It could be a small roof leak, or some bad windows, but it could be inadequate overall ventilation which may have allowed condensation to start rot in several places. If you smell furniture polish and coffee or fresh baking, be pleased – but also cautious – that you may be in the hands of a good salesman. How, and how well, is the barge insulated? Do the windows (or below them) show signs of condensation?

Is the overall layout both sensible and suitable for your purposes? Does it have enough of the right types of room? Will it sleep enough people? Is there enough headroom? Can any shortcomings in this area be fixed without too much effort?

What fitted furniture is there? What loose furniture will come with it? Can you get your furniture in?

Does the domestic equipment it comes with suit you? You can usually replace this later, but that will be another cost. Does it have other features you particularly want (a fireplace, for example)?

6.1.3 ENGINE ROOM

Go into the engine room. What is your first impression? Is it easy to get into? Is all the machinery readily reachable? Are you sufficiently protected from the dangerous bits? If it is grubby and untidy, take note.

What type of engine and drive does it have? Is this what you want?

Are there signs of fluid leaks (not just damp, look for vertical rust streaks too) or temporary repairs?

Generally, if it looks as if a certain Heath Robinson (well known in the barge world) did the plumbing or wiring, you have got a case which needs the advice of an expert. Make sure all pipes and cables are properly secured to the hull or the engine, that the rubber fittings are not perished and that the jubilee clips (metal bands which clamp the ends of hoses in place) still allow opening and fastening.

Check the water in the engine header tank. If it looks murky and greasy this could indicate a problem with the cylinder head gasket or the cylinder head itself. Check there is sufficient antifreeze in the cooling water (you need a special tester for this – inexpensive and you may already have one for your car). If not, the engine might have frost damage from a previous cold winter.

Look at the fuel tanks (often in the engine room). Are they in good condition? Are they big enough?

Is the exhaust wet or dry? If it is dry, the muffler and the exhaust pipes should be well lagged. How is the engine cooled?

Ask for the engine to be started. Does it fire up without problem? Does it smoke (let it warm up before deciding as most diesels smoke when cold)? Does it make strange noises?

If the vendor does not want to take the barge out for a short trip (not necessarily an unreasonable position), ask him to run the drive at the mooring in forward and reverse under at least medium throttle. (Check first that the barge is securely moored and that the propeller wash will not carry away any other boats, waterfowl nests, etc..) Any problems going into gear? Any nasty noises or vibration?

When the engine has been turned off, go back into the engine room. Any signs of distress (leaks, strange smells)?

Always ask to see the log when evaluating the engine. A conscientious owner will have kept a detailed record of engine maintenance and repairs, which can tell a very meaningful tale. No log? Be a little suspicious of any claims made concerning rebuilds, etc..

No matter what engine you find in a barge which appeals to you (and this applies to other major equipment on board too, particularly the transmission), it is worth checking on the supply of parts, including whether they are (still) available at all for this make and model, and whether the distributors are conveniently located (considering your own cruising plans).

6.1.4 SYSTEMS

Get the vendor to describe each system to you in turn. If the person on hand cannot do that, ask him to find you someone who can. If no one can, be worried (who has been doing the maintenance?).

Look at each system in turn. Is the wiring/piping tidy, in good materials, properly supported, and (gas and electricity) not in the bilge?

Regarding the electrical systems: are there adequate and accessible circuit breakers (or fuses, not uncommon in older installations) with labels? Are the batteries accessible, full of electrolyte, and free of salts on the terminals? When were they installed? What is the capacity of the batteries, inverter, generator? Does the generator start easily, sound healthy, and not smoke? Try every light and appliance, and get clear explanations of anything which is not working. Turn on a couple of heavy electrical loads at once for a few minutes (if the system is intended to stand it) and see if any circuits trip. Be suspicious if any of these tests fails.

Look at the domestic water pump, and listen to it run. Is the flow adequate from the taps, particularly with more than one on? Look at the tank. Is it in good condition externally? Is the water inside clean? Is it big enough?

How is the sewage handled? Is the holding tank big enough? What is it made of, and what is its condition? Is there a disposal pump, and is it working properly?

How is the barge heated? Ask for the heating to be fired up, even in summer, and check that the circulation system is functional. Is there adequate ventilation to whatever is burning?

Check for all required safety and navigation equipment. Do the lights, horn, radio etc. all work?

What type of steering is installed? Does the system look well maintained (i.e. are cables greased and taut, are there any signs of leaking hydraulic fluid)?

6.2 DOCUMENTS

Ask to see the ship's papers. You should look for the following.

6.2.1 PROOF OF OWNERSHIP

Proof of ownership varies from country to country and will need to be checked fully if the purchase proceeds. For now, just ask to see whatever proof there is. If nothing can be produced, or if it looks unconvincing, or if it is in names you do not recognise, ask questions.

6.2.2 DESCRIPTION

Many vessels have some form of gauging document. In the Netherlands, all trading barges had to have the *Meetbrief.* Even an out-of-date one is useful for verifying dimensions.

6.2.3 SURVEYS

You will (no exceptions, please!) need to get any craft you are serious about resurveyed by your own surveyor before completing purchase. But start by asking to see any reports of previous surveys. When was the survey done? What was the hull thickness (there should be a plan showing the thickness found at each testing point)? What problems were found by the surveyor, and can the vendor show that they were properly remedied?

Be careful here. Just because a barge has been surveyed does not mean that it has passed any tests of acceptability. A survey is not a guarantee of good condition; it is simply an inspection by an expert. The survey may have found the barge to be in terrible shape.

6.2.4 CERTIFICATES

Many national jurisdictions and navigation authorities require craft to be inspected periodically for safety etc. Ask to see any certificates that this barge has. Are they current? If not, why not?

6.2.5 LOGS

Not every barge owner keeps a log of any kind. But many do, not only of cruises but also of maintenance. Ask to see any that are available.

Has much work been done? Are there any recurring problems? Have reputable traders been used? Are the bills available to substantiate log entries?

Your investigations may be hampered by language difficulties, or simply by a desire not to intrude and appear too suspicious in the presence of congenial owner-occupiers. The results should still be valuable, though.

Even if you are no expert, at the end of the inquisition you should be able to form a reasonable idea of the overall condition of the barge. Problems of condition do not, of course, rule out a purchase, as the barge may be one you particularly like. But at least you will be going ahead with your eyes open wider and perhaps be better able to compare this barge with others and to consider the reasonableness of the asking price.

Keep your notes safe. Otherwise you will surely soon be confused as to which barge was the one with the thin stern plates and which one had the leaking fuel tank.

7 THE PURCHASE TRANSACTION

You have flown to the Netherlands several times. You have slogged around a slew of boatyards, always in the rain it seems. You have looked at rust buckets (only just about floating, thanks to pumps), vessels with conversions that defy all logic or aesthetics, and beautiful ships beyond even the budget of your dreams. But finally, just the right barge has appeared. You have decided to take the plunge. But how?

Like any financial transaction, a barge purchase can be handled in many ways. We will describe what we think is good practice, but there may be sound reasons for variation in particular cases.

A lot of money is about to change hands, so formality and attention to detail are vital. Do not get rushed by fear of losing the deal. Do not accept unsubstantiated statements about important matters. Remember, while you have got the money, you are in the driver's (helmsman's?) seat.

There are two ways you might proceed.

One is to make the offer fairly general and 'subject to contract', and negotiate detailed terms of the purchase after you have an indication from the vendor that your offer may be acceptable. The other is to make the offer so complete that it is effectively a contract itself once a few blanks (particularly the vendor's name and signature!) are filled in. The latter has many appeals. It can speed up negotiation and processing in general, and it can prevent gazumping. We will assume this is the route you will follow, but if you do not, items which we suggest but which you leave out of the offer should probably appear in the final contract.

Beware, though. If you do make the offer quite complete, it is likely to become a binding agreement if the vendor accepts it in full and signs it. That is a major strength of this approach. But it means that you should be sure your offer is serious. You might otherwise find you are buying a barge when you thought you were merely testing the water.

We cover the purchase process assuming you will go through the following steps: offer, acceptance, survey, completion. We also suggest how you might get some professional help if you need it.

7.1 THE OFFER

To get things off to a firm start, you should make an offer to purchase, and we suggest you make it as clear and complete as possible.

7.1.1 PUT IT IN WRITING

The offer should definitely be in writing, with your witnessed signature and the date. This does several things for you. It makes it clear that an offer has actually been made. It establishes when it was made, which can help prevent delays in presenting it to the owner by, for example, an agent who would like to solicit and present an alternative offer first. It shows you are serious. It makes it less likely that the terms of your offer will be misunderstood.

On this last point, by all means write up your offer in English, no matter in which country the barge is being sold. You may find yourself much better off if the offer (and contract, if there is one) is in your language. If you are working with a broker, he will be able to translate it for the vendor if necessary. Even if you aren't, almost any vendor in Europe will know someone who can do so. But do make sure that the vendor gets a copy of the original along with any translation, and that you get a copy of the translation.

7.1.2 WHAT ARE YOU BUYING?

The offer should identify as exactly as possible the barge you are offering to buy. Refer to a registration number if possible. Otherwise, describe the vessel and where and when you saw it in enough detail to avoid any possibility of mistaken identity (or even substitution).

Specify an inventory of what you expect to come with the barge in the way of equipment, furniture, etc.. You do not want to show up on acceptance day and find that there is no longer a dinghy to take you to the mooring buoy and, when you get there, that the sophisticated radio system has vanished.

7.1.3 WHAT ARE YOU PAYING?

Set out exactly what payment you are offering in total, and in what currency. Detail when the payment would be made. Do you want to make payment in three stages? Say so, and how. Do you have to get the money out of a term deposit in the Cayman Islands and have it changed into guilders? Make sure you leave yourself enough time to do this, preferably stated relative to some clear event in the process.

Remember, the amount you propose and all the conditions constitute an *offer*. By all means pitch it as far below the asking price as you think you can get away with, but expect to negotiate.

You should expect to put down a deposit right away if your offer is accepted. Say how much you are proposing (10% may be reasonable), who will hold it, and what happens to it – both if the purchase goes to completion and if it does not. Take this into account in your payment terms.

Make it clear who will pay each broker involved, and when.

7.1.4 WHAT'S THE DEAL?

You will not be proposing just to put down your money and cruise away. There will always be other conditions you will want met. All of these should be set out in the offer.

SURVEY

One condition should always be 'Subject to survey and the vessel being in an insurable condition'. You should set out your right to have a suitable survey done by someone of your choice, and also the timing for getting the survey done (including the vendor making the barge available at an appropriate location), who pays for it, and what happens as a result of it. Because this is so vital, we go into it in more detail later.

Usual practice is for the purchaser to pay for the survey and docking or slipping needed to carry it out. (*Read the comments on obligations below carefully.*)

TITLE

Title to the vessel, and the right of the vendor to sell it, should be satisfactorily substantiated. All liens and other claims on the vessel must be cleared, and warranted to have been cleared, by the vendor as part of completion.

You should require that title be transferred to you as part of completion. It can be a good idea to set timing for this. You should insist on provision by the vendor of a properly signed bill of sale.

REGISTRATION

The barge may be on a register when you see it. You may need to have it removed from that register, or instruct that it be re-registered in your name. If so, you should make timely execution by the vendor of the documents necessary to do this a condition of the offer.

OTHER

You may require other points to be confirmed, for example, that the vessel's size falls within certain specified dimensions, if this is crucial to you. This can be confirmed during the survey.

7.1.5 OBLIGATIONS

Specify what happens after acceptance. Who has to do what by when? If something is not done on time, do you or the vendor have the right to break things off? What happens then to the deposit? Must the vendor reimburse your expenses if he cries off?

The usual arrangements are as follows. If you withdraw arbitrarily (i.e. for a reason other than covered by a condition in the offer) or fail to complete in time, the vendor can cancel the contract and keep both your deposit and his barge. If he withdraws arbitrarily or fails to complete, you can cancel the contract and he should pay all your expenses of docking and surveying and a further set sum or percentage to offset your legal or notary fees and travel expenses, your wasted time, and the possibility that you missed buying another barge in the meantime.

7.1.6 KEEP IT SHORT

The document should state how long the offer remains open. A few days should be enough in most cases.

7.1.7 THE DOTTED LINE

It should have a space for the vendor to sign his acceptance and to have his signature dated and witnessed. It should require that the signed document be delivered to you at a specified address within a specified short time of signing.

7.2 ASSISTANCE

If you feel all this is a bit out of your depth, get professional help.

In the UK, it could be a lawyer (but finding one familiar with buying barges in mainland Europe is quite a trick).

In the Netherlands, you can use a notary who (for a few hundred pounds, of course) will help you draw up the documents (offer and/or contract), do the title and lien searches, execute the ownership transfer, and handle the registration. Dutch notaries are professionally independent, so it is all right to use one suggested by the vendor's broker.

If you would like to avoid professional fees, obtain a copy of the sample *Agreement for the Sale and Purchase of a Second-Hand Vessel* published by the British Marine Industries Federation (BMIF). This may not exactly fit your case, but can be a useful guide to wording your own document.

7.3 ACCEPTANCE

Your initial offer will quite likely be rejected. The vendor may not like your price, or may not be willing to go along with one or more of your conditions. If this is the case, try to get him to make you a counter-offer; in effect, to say he will accept your offer if certain points are changed. The advantage of this is that it allows all the non-contentious points in your offer to be accepted and put to one side. Any further negotiations can focus on the key issues.

With luck, after haggling, you will arrive at an agreement. As soon as this is signed by the vendor, and any amendments initialled by you, the clock starts to run again – you have to organise the survey and perhaps your financing.

7.4 THE SURVEY

7.4.1 WHY YOU HAVE TO HAVE ONE

There is no question. The vessel must be surveyed afresh by a surveyor of your choice before purchase. Do not accept as sufficient a survey report produced by the owner or broker, no matter how recent.

It should be obvious that you need a survey for your own protection, but there is a second reason. You probably will not get insurance cover without presenting a survey report drawn up by a surveyor with acceptable qualifications.

7.4.2 CHOOSING YOUR SURVEYOR

Try to find a surveyor who is skilled, independent and particular about detail. Make sure he is acceptable to your insurer. You want him to find and report the faults, and to advise you on their significance and what is needed to remedy them. Even if a broker is working for you, be cautious about accepting his recommendation of a surveyor. After all, the broker's prime motive is to get the deal to completion; that might conflict with ensuring you know all the problems. He just might suggest a surveyor he has a cosy relationship with ... Get a list of several surveyors, with some suggested by independent parties.

Check out your potential surveyors for qualifications and for experience with barges in particular, and for reputation if possible. Talk to at least a couple of preferred ones, to get a feel for what they will do for you and whether you are impressed by their knowledge and approach. This is also a good way to build up a relationship with your surveyor, which often helps a lot in getting a good job done and good advice. You do not have to use a native surveyor (a number of British surveyors regularly survey barges in mainland Europe).

If your surveyor is accredited to issue UK Boat Safety Certificates, you may be able to save yourself a second (safety) survey when you take the barge to Britain. It is likely that only a British surveyor will have this qualification.

7.4.3 WHAT'S IN A SURVEY?

You (not the vendor, broker, or anyone else) should instruct the surveyor. The surveyor will ask you to sign a contract setting out what you expect of him and he of you. Make it clear what you want him to do, and by when. Ascertain the surveyor's fee before signing and be sure to specify if you want a market valuation or an estimate of repair costs for any defects he finds (he may charge an extra fee for this). You may want to familiarise yourself with a surveying code of practice (the Yacht Designers & Surveyors Association produces one but there are others) before the discussion.

The most important element of the survey is inspection of the hull. Usual practice is for the surveyor to check sufficient representative areas for thickness and soundness. The process should start with the hull being pressure-washed, which the buyer usually pays for. The surveyor will then normally have to scrape off external coatings (paint, bitumen, etc.) in small areas to make tests, but he usually has a pot of suitable coating to hand to make these spots good afterwards. He will also check inside the hull, expecting to move equipment and perhaps to do some minor dismantling. Make sure the vendor is happy .

There should also be an interior inspection to identify and gauge the adequacy and condition of the barge's systems. The survey will normally include an engine check, but you should not expect the surveyor to look into or comment on the engine's innards. Because you cannot assume that the engine is 'surveyed', you may want to get a further assessment of it from an engineer or mechanic.

In some cases it may not be feasible for the surveyor to run up the engine or other systems (if the barge has been decommissioned for example). Be prepared to be flexible, while still getting as much assurance as you can.

7.4.4 DOING THE SURVEYING

The barge must be out of the water for the hull inspection, in a dry dock or on a tidal grid providing ready access for the surveyor to the bottom and the stern gear. Not all docks give the surveyor good working conditions. Ask your surveyor for a list of ones he recommends, or at least for his comments on one you are thinking of using.

The interior check is usually better done while the barge is afloat. (Think how difficult it is to test the engine if the propeller is not in water!) This can be a logistical difficulty, as you may want any underwater work done after the survey while the barge is still docked, so it can be a good idea for the internal check to be done first. This may mean the surveyor has to make two visits. Discuss this with him in advance.

A surveyor is likely to work better if not harassed. You do not need to be there to get a good result. If you really want to be on hand, ensure you do not hinder the surveyor or interrupt him too often. It can be best to meet him when he is nearly finished so he can show you anything significant he has found.

Perhaps more important is to make sure the vendor is not there. It may be in the vendor's interest to distract your surveyor. He may be offended at the suggestion that anything is wrong with his barge or disagree with the significance of any shortcomings the surveyor finds. If the vendor insists he will not let the survey proceed without his presence, suggest that he send someone whom he trusts but who is emotionally neutral in his place, with instructions simply to provide access (e.g. keys) as required and to make sure that the surveyor does not damage the vessel.

7.4.5 THE SURVEY REPORT

After the inspections, the surveyor needs time to consider his findings and to write his report. Expect him to take up to a week. Once you have read the report, he should make himself available to discuss with you any questions it may raise. If you have chosen the right surveyor and have formed a good relationship with him, he will probably be a source of very good advice not only on how any faults might be remedied, but also as to the possible cost of this, who might best do it for you, and even on the desirability and value of the vessel. Do not forget though that you are getting an opinion based on experience, not a valuer's appraisal.

What will you see in the report? For the hull, and for each major interior aspect, there should be an overall assessment and then a detailed list of any defects found. The surveyor will usually grade these as to seriousness and urgency for remedy, often indicating which must be done right away or in the near future.

7.4.6 THE RESULTS OF THE SURVEY

Now we have gone through what the survey will cover, it is time to consider what conditions concerning it you might want in your purchase agreement.

It is usual to expect the vendor to make good at his expense any significant shortcomings the survey reveals which had not been made known previously, while maintaining the agreed purchase price. However, there are some provisos. The vendor will usually expect the right to cancel the contract without penalty if the work required by the survey would cost more than a stated percentage of the purchase price (typically 10%). The purchaser can, of course, agree to fund any work beyond this amount.

On the other hand, if the barge turns out not to be economically repairable, or if the vendor refuses to pay for the repairs the surveyor specifies (even within the agreed percentage), the contract should specify that you get all your deposit back and compensation.

Dealing with equipment – whether it is there, is adequate, and works properly – is fairly straightforward. Hull considerations, however, are probably less familiar to you although they are the most important.

The minimum insurable hull thickness is 3mm. But you would not want a barge that was only that thick. Your contract should normally require a minimum thickness of 4mm. This is usually interpreted as meaning a ruling thickness of 4mm, with minor localised pitting in a few areas allowable. The report should include a thickness map, showing measurements scattered over the entire bottom and underwater sides of the barge. In his text the surveyor will usually comment on this map, and identify any suspect or downright thin areas for attention. He should also indicate any seams, rivets, dents, etc. which he thinks need repairing. Your contract should make it clear that remedying all this will be at the cost of the vendor.

But in case some areas are too thin, you need to specify how this will be fixed. The usual practice is to overplate, i.e. to weld on a patch of new metal which will cover the entire area concerned. Many barges have such patches, and if they are done properly they are entirely acceptable. Be a little dubious if they cover very large areas, though, and ask the surveyor if he thinks they are properly fastened to the hull. A second layer of overplating is not a good idea. If the first overplating is now thin, it and the original plating underneath should probably come off and be replaced by new plate. This can be a tricky and expensive job.

Overplating needs to be carried out properly. If you have the work done at a reputable yard and ask your surveyor to help you commission it, results will normally be fine.

A big question is, 'How thick should the new plate be?' You might think the answer is '4mm' because that is all thickness needed. Not so. Since most of the cost of overplating is in the welder's labour and the docking, it makes sense to go to 6mm for the extra life it will have. Try to get this into the contract. If the vendor really balks, you may get him to accept 5mm. If he refuses to go up at all, it may be worth your paying for the extra weight of steel. It is usually a good investment.

7.4.7 COMPLETION

You have a contract, the survey has been carried out, the required work has been commissioned at the vendor's expense, and you have arranged your financing. You are all ready to close the deal.

Here you really do need a lawyer or notary. He may already be holding your deposit. He can certainly hold the balance while the papers are processed.

He can check that all conditions of the contract have been complied with, prepare any necessary forms, arrange for signatures, and file everything official.

With luck, everyone is smiling. Hands are shaken, a celebratory glass or two emptied. Congratulations, you have a barge. But do remember to put all your new keys and the essential papers somewhere safe before you get too jolly!

8 YOU'VE BOUGHT IT, NOW WHAT?

You are now a barge owner. This means you are now responsible for this large object floating at someone else's mooring. What are you going to do with it?

Our first answer to this question is that you should not start from here. You should take several steps before completion day, and you should start on them as soon as you are confident that the sale really is going to go through.

8.1 GETTING READY FOR OWNERSHIP

8.1.1 INSURANCE

As soon as the barge becomes yours, it is at your risk. Not just the risks of fire, theft, of sinking but also liability for any damage it might do to someone else or his property if, for example, it broke loose from its moorings.

You need insurance from day one. Well before ownership day, you should have approached at least two or three insurers, giving them a description of the barge and of your plans for it, and asking for quotes. By the great day, you should have chosen your insurer, and have cover in place.

Insurers are used to this situation, and are usually helpful and flexible in setting up cover quickly and recognising that the cover may need to be adjusted before too long as, for example, work is done on the barge, it comes into commission, or it is moved to another country.

A comparative survey of barge insurers is published periodically in *Blue Flag*.

8.1.2 MOORING

If you have not made arrangements with the landlord of the mooring the barge is occupying on ownership day, you may find you are in trespass or subject to unwelcome charges.

In most cases, you may be able to negotiate an extension of the agreement under which the vendor was keeping the barge there. This can be helpful in giving you some time to get things better organised. However, do think about whether you actually want to keep your new possession there. The mooring may be too exposed to weather, the effects of passing traffic, or predation by the help-yourself brigade. It may be too expensive.

If you have, or want, to move the barge to another temporary location immediately you own it, you may be able to locate short-term moorings not too far away. Short-term moorings are usually not nearly so difficult to find as good long-term ones. Ask around locally, ask the vendor, ask the broker. The mooring charges may still be higher than you like (although in some areas free short-term moorings can be found), but at least you will be legal.

8.1.3 REGISTRATION

If the barge is registered in one country, but is sold to a national of another country, it is normal practice to de-register it. A vessel may be registered only to a national, a nationally registered company, or a resident foreigner, in most EU countries.

It may be a temptation to maintain the foreign registration by using an accommodation address in the country concerned, perhaps to avoid the costs of registering it at home. However, if your barge is shorter than 24m, it can be put on the UK Small Ship Registry (SSR) at relatively low cost. This produces ships' papers acceptable throughout Europe. However, the SSR is not a registry of title so cannot be used to confirm ownership or liens. The SSR is currently operated by the UK government's Maritime and Coastguard Agency (MCA – formerly MSA – see Appendix 1 for address). If your vessel is over 24m, you may register it with the British Registry of Shipping. This is not compulsory and is a costly and lengthy business relative to the SSR.

You will almost certainly need to register the vessel with the navigation authority for the waters you will keep it on. This puts you on the authority's books for levying navigation charges etc. Contact the offices of the authority for the relevant forms, and get the paperwork completed before the barge shows up at the entry point or it may be refused admission.

8.1.4 FAMILIARISATION

Particularly with a sophisticated conversion, a barge is a complex object. It has a lot of systems, and quirks. It needs to be maintained and operated properly if equipment is to do what it should and to have a reasonable life. How can you avoid getting things expensively wrong when you take over?

If you can, and if he knows anything, get close to the vendor or even an owner before him. Find out if he has any useful written information such as receipts, manuals, suppliers' addresses, wiring and plumbing diagrams: insist they are all given to you. Ask him to go through the barge with you in detail, explaining everything, what it does, where it is, how it works, what supplies it needs, what replacement parts should be kept on hand, what you must and must not do, how to handle any common problems. Keep asking questions until you are comfortable. Take copious notes. If the barge is mobile, ask him to go on a short cruise with you. Watch carefully, ask more questions, take more notes.

If no suitable former owner is available, try and find someone else to advise you in the same way. Your surveyor might do it (perhaps at a price), or might be able to recommend someone else. Do you have any barge-owning friends who seem to know a thing or two? If you will be having work done on the barge right away, can the boatyard owner be of any use?

The information you get is of great value to you. Treat it with respect. File it properly and safely. You might even assemble it into your personal *Barge Operators Manual*, which you can update as you gain knowledge or change things on board.

At the same time, start a log for the barge. This should cover not only details of your journeys, but also all your equipment purchases, maintenance and repairs. Keeping a log is very worthwhile. Not only will it help you recall your cruising experiences, it will keep track of your expenditures, and is a most useful tool for trouble-shooting, by answering questions such as: Has this problem happened before? What did I do in the period just before it happened? Is this piece of equipment still under guarantee?

Quite apart from anything else, documentation such as this will make the barge easier to sell later. Remember how you wanted to see it when you were buying?

Despite all this, you are still at the bottom of a steep learning curve. Ready yourself for a string of glitches or hitches in your first year or two of ownership. Each of these will teach you something worthwhile, and you will soon be discussing batteries and toilet systems with the best of them.

8.1.5 SAFETY CERTIFICATION

Before you can register with the navigation authority whose waters you wish to keep your barge on, and in some cases (particularly in the UK) before you can enter its waters, the authority may insist that your get a specified safety certificate for the vessel. In Britain, this will probably be the BSS (Boat Safety Scheme). Obtaining this requires a(nother) survey, by someone accredited by the scheme. But this inspection can be done while the barge is afloat, it is not usually too expensive, and the certificate is good for several years. Principal checks cover gas and fuel systems, etc., and can result in immediate remedial work being required.

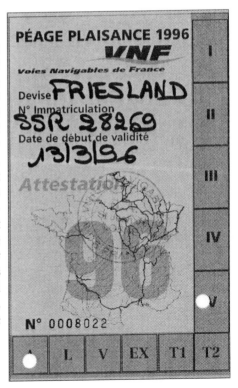

Complying with such a scheme is not an unreasonable requirement. Would *you* want to share a lock with a vessel with bilges full of gas?

Barges bought in mainland Europe frequently do not meet UK safety standards. The compliance work required can range from minimal (such as buying a couple of fire extinguishers) to major (re-doing all the gas piping). The rules are technical and voluminous. The usual practice in the UK is to get a preliminary inspection by a BSS surveyor so any faults noted can be dealt with before the real survey is done. However, it can be difficult to find someone familiar with the BSS rules in central France, say, although one or two barge surveyors working in mainland Europe are also familiar with BSS and might be able to give you an indication of the work needed.

In the UK, it would be reasonable to specify 'Must pass BSS' as a condition of purchase, but you probably would not get away with that on the other side of the Channel.

8.1.6 ALTERATIONS OR REPAIRS

We cannot go into all the ins and outs of repairs here, but there are one or two points you might want to consider.

In many cases, the buyer moves straight from the purchase to the boatyard. There is usually some work you want to have done right away, and anyway the survey may have revealed some things that must be attended to immediately.

Underwater work (plating over thin hull spots, replacement of the stern bushing, etc.) can be done most economically while the barge is still on the slip after the survey, so it makes sense to choose a slip in a yard with a good reputation and price list for such work. That yard may also be a good choice for doing the other jobs, and you may get a lower total bill if all the work is done at the same place. However, once the barge is afloat again (and, presumably, mobile) your freedom of choice returns, so do shop around.

If you have bought the barge in mainland Europe, but will be taking it to England, you have the very basic choice of whether to have the work done there or here. Many Dutch yards are very experienced in working with barges, and will readily do work that an English yard would shun. However, against this, Dutch standards can be quite different from English ones, and it is harder to monitor what is going on from another country. We do not plump for either choice here, just mention that it bears consideration. You could even have the more standard work (e.g. hull repairs) done by one yard on the mainland then bring the barge to Britain for any new systems and interior refitting (which usually benefit from greater owner attention).

8.1.7 HANDLING YOUR PURCHASE

All this, and you have hardly, perhaps not at all, been at the wheel yet. And if, as is not unusual, this is your first foray into barging, you may be getting a few butterflies thinking about taking charge of that metal monster which looks bigger each time you see it. Particularly if it is currently moored near some expensive plastic.

Cheer up. Most barges handle well. But, like anything else, steering them is something you have to learn. And the only way to learn it is to do it. But not necessarily on your own barge or, at least, not for the first bit.

Perhaps the pleasantest way to learn is to get invited to cruise on other people's barges. This is not necessarily the imposition you might think. Many barge skippers need crew every now and then, and may be glad of the company. Make your needs known to other owners and you may be pleasantly surprised. After all, they all had to start once, and remembering their own experiences tends to make them sympathetic.

Another option is to pay for training. A few owners offer first-time steerers training on their own barges for a fee. Sometimes this simply involves going out for a few afternoons. Other operators may make it part of a holiday cruise of a week or more.

We suggested earlier that you get the vendor to take you out. This is a good way to try out your own barge with someone familiar with it on hand, and is highly recommended even for a trip of only an hour or two. Perhaps the vendor might even like to come along for a day or two on your first trip to say 'goodbye' to his old friend? It does happen, and he might be very happy to be invited.

At the very least, when you move your barge for the first time, take along a couple of crew experienced in such matters. If you have not got any friends in this category, you can usually find someone with the right skills who will do it for a fee, and who will probably be willing to give you a steering lesson along the way. To find such a person, ask the broker, the vendor, and generally in the locality. Or contact your friendly Barge Association!

A British keel locks through in France

8.2 GETTING IT HOME

Bringing your new purchase home to the U.K. from darkest Belgium may be a challenge you are looking forward to. But some buyers cannot stand that much excitement, or simply may not have the time for the trip. And in any case, crossing the Channel requires special care and may involve substantial delay waiting for the right weather. But what do you do then if you are planning to move on board in six weeks, and you have already sold your house!

Get someone to deliver the barge for you. This service is readily available, frequently offered by people with a lot of barging experience and a good track record. Once again, inquire from the usual sources. But if you do plan to use such a service, make tentative arrangements as far in advance as possible to ensure your chosen skipper will be available when you need him. The price for a delivery depends on the length of the trip, and whether a Channel crossing is involved. However, it is unlikely to be less than £1,000, and may be a multiple of that. Surprisingly, it may also be possible to have your barge brought home by truck. There are specialist haulage companies which can move vessels of 22m or even longer. Obviously a big crane is needed at each end of the journey

Before you set out, be sure to check your insurance. Some insurers require an extra premium for a channel crossing and may have other requirements such as using a qualified skipper.

CONCLUSION

When we first read this handbook in draft, we wondered why anyone would go through all the hassle we had documented. In fact, we wondered how we had got through it when we became owners. And it was that which made us realise that it looks much more troublesome on paper than it often proves in practice. As you pass through the process, it all tends to make sense. The advice we offer will probably seem like minor steering corrections at the time.

Despite all the potential pitfalls, the process itself can be absorbing, even fun. After all, it usually involves travelling to interesting and unfamiliar (often unsuspected) places, meeting fascinating people, and messing around in boats. Some people pay a lot of money for holidays which involve little more.

Ah yes, paying a lot of money. Well, that does come into it, of course. But if you take things cautiously and sensibly, it should prove to be money well spent. You will end up with something which, whether or not it turns out to be a sound investment in the financial sense (opinions are somewhat divided about the merits of barges in this respect), should bring enormous enjoyment into your life. And that is something you certainly can't say about everything you buy.

We encourage you to try it. We would be pleased to hear how you have done.

We wish you the best of luck.

APPENDIX 1 – CONTACTS

UK addresses unless shown otherwise. Phone numbers as dialled from the UK. An extensive contacts list of inland waterways authorities and other organisations appears in *Canalmanac*, a pamphlet published annually by Waterways World magazine (*see next page*).

Government Bodies:

British Waterways Board (BWB)
Willow Grange, Church Road
Watford WD1 3QA
Tel. 01923 226422

Environment Agency (EA)
Kings Meadow Road
Reading RG1 8DQ
Tel. 01734 535520

Registry of Shipping and Seamen
Maritime and Coastguard Agency (MCA)
PO Box 165
Cardiff CF4 5FU
Tel. 01222 747333

Voies Navigables de France (VNF)
175 rue Ludovic Boutleux
62400 Béthune
France
Tel. 00 33 [0]3 21 63 24 54

Organisations:

Dutch Barge Association (DBA)
Port Werburgh, Vicarage Lane
Hoo, Rochester ME3 9TW
Tel. 07000 BARGES (07000 227437)

Inland Waterways Association (IWA)
114 Regent's Park Road
London NW1 8UQ
Tel. 0171 586 2556

Residential Boat Owners Association (RBOA)
Box 181
Macclesfield SK11 0NT
Tel. 0181 846 9287

Royal Yachting Association (RYA)
Romsey Road, Eastleigh SO50 9YA
Tel. 01703 627400

SURVEYORS & CONSULTING ENGINEERS
Institute of Marine Engineers (IMarE) Small Ship Group 'A' Register
Secretary: K Anderson, 76 Mark Lane, London EC3R 7JN
Tel. 0171 481 8493

Yacht Designers & Surveyors Association (YDSA)
Secretary: Rae Boxall, Wheelhouse, Petersfield Road, White Hill
Borden, Hants GU35 9BYU

Cadastre Offices in the Netherlands

The Cadastre registers immovable property where legal ownership is recorded. It also registers ships in the Netherlands and has kept a shipping register since 1838.

The principal offices are listed below (there are also many sub-offices). Initial enquiries regarding a barge should be made to one of these.

Groningen Cadastre
Kempkensberg, 9722 TB, Groningen or PO Box 413, 9700 AK, Groningen
Tel. 00 31 (050) 520 84 31 Fax 00 31 (050) 525 46 24

Limburg Cadastre
Bredeweg 239. 6043 GA, Roermond or PO Box 1075, 6040 KB, Roermond
Tel. 00 31 (0475) 39 11 25 Fax 00 31 (0475) 32 4 41

Amsterdam Cadastre
Prins Hendrikkade 33, 1012 TM, Amsterdam
or PO Box 1242, 1000 BE, Amsterdam
Tel. 00 31 (020) 42 22 12 Fax 00 31 (020) 42 29 87

Gelderland Cadastre
Groningensingel 21, 6835 EA,
Arnhem or
PO Box 9015, 6800 Arnhem
Tel. 00 31 (026) 322 62 8 Fax
00 31 (026) 322 63 41

Rotterdam Cadastre
Westzeedijk 507, 3024 EL,
Rotterdam
Tel. 00 31 (010) 448 13 81
Fax 00 31 (010) 425 73 19

Periodicals

Boats and Planes for Sale (*monthly magazine*)
44A North Street
Chichester, West Sussex
Tel. 01243 533394

Fluvial (*bi-monthly magazine*)
64 rue Jean-Jaques Rousseau
21000 Dijon
France
00 33 [0]3 80 73 39 39

Jacht & Bootgid (*bi-monthly magazine, Dutch version of Boats & Planes,
with English and list of brokers*)
Postbus 1
NL 8265 ZK Oppenhuizen
Holland
00 31 515 559803

Loot (*daily paper*)
24 Kilburn Road
London NW6 5TF
Tel. 0171 625 0266

Weekblad Schuttevaer (*weekly newspaper*)
Leeuwenbrug 99
Postbus 23
7400 GA Deventer
Netherlands
Tel. 00 31 570 64 88 10
E-mail 101471.211@compuserve.com

Waterways World (*monthly magazine*)
The Well House, High Street
Burton-on-Trent DE14 1JQ
Tel. 01283 742970

Blue Flag (*quarterly journal with many relevant articles*)
Dutch Barge Association
Port Werburgh, Vicarage Lane
Hoo, Kent ME3 9TW
Tel. 07000 BARGES (07000 227437)

APPENDIX 11 – BIBLIOGRAPHY

Books

Through the French Canals by Philip Bristow, pub. Adlard Coles Nautical. This book has probably tempted more people to explore French waterways than has any other.

Slow Boat through Germany by Hugh McKnight, Adlard Coles Nautical 1993.

Through the German Waterways by Philip Bristow, pub. Adlard Coles Nautical.

Sell up and Sail by Bill & Laurel Cooper, pub. Adlard Coles Nautical, 1997.

Watersteps through France – to the Camargue by canal by Bill & Laurel Cooper.

Watersteps round Europe – Greece to England by barge by Bill & Laurel Cooper 2300-mile voyage from Greece home via Ionian Isles, Corsica, France.

Back Door to Byzantium by Bill & Laurel Cooper. Witty account of dangerous journey from the North Sea to the Black Sea.

The European Waterways by Marian Martin, pub. Adlard Coles Nautical, 1997 Manual for first-time users. Regulations for cruising in Europe.

Barging About in France by T & D Murrell, pub. DBA £2.50 A pamphlet on what you need to know.

European Regulations for Inland Waterways by Marian Martin, pub. Adlard Coles Nautical, 1998. The CEVNI rules in English.

Code Vagnon Fluvial by Henri Vagnon £10 Regulations for cruising in France and information for gaining PP Licence (in French, annual publication).

Tests Vagnon "Riviere" £9.50 Self assessment test papers for PP test (in French)

Vagnon Carte de Plaisance £8.50 Simplified code primarily for hirers on French canals. (in English but not adequate by itself for PP test).

Available from the DBA

Books *continued*

Habiter une Péniche by Bernard Lécluse, pub. La Maison Fluviale, Dijon, 1996.
Buying, converting and living on barges in France (in French).

ANWB (Dutch Tourist Board), Almanak voor Watertoerisme 1 and 11 (annual)

The Dutch Barge Book by David Evershed, 89 Atlantic Way, Porthtowan,
Truro, Cornwall, TR4 8AH.
History and descriptions of Dutch sailing barges, in English.

France the Quiet Way by John Liley, pub. Stanford Maritime, 1975.
A knowledgeable and amusing account of buying a Leeds & Liverpool short
boat and taking it through France.

Barge Country by John Liley, pub. Stanford Maritime, 1980.
The author trades his short boat for a klipper to explore the Netherlands.

Slow Boat through France by Hugh McKnight, pub. David & Charles, 1991.
'The French boater's bible' with practical, historic and tourist information.

Travels with Lionel by Hart Massey, pub. Victor Gollancz, 1988. A retired and
inexperienced couple buy, convert and cruise a barge in France.

Barging in Europe by Roger van Dyken, pub. Cedarbrook, Lyndon WA, 1997.

Maps & Guides

Ordnance Survey Guide to the Waterways, pub. Robert Nicholson.

Inland Waterways of England & Wales (map by L. Edwards),
pub. Imray Laurie Norie & Wilson.

Inland Cruising Map of England for Larger Craft, Stanford Maritime.

Navicartes, pub. Éditions Cartographiques Maritimes.

Inland Waterways of France, pub. Imray Laurie Norie & Wilson.
Map of France plus most important Belgian and Dutch waterways.

Guides Vagnon de Tourisme Fluvial, pub. Les Éditions du Plaisancier.

Sportschiffahrtskarten, Nautische Veröffentlichungen (Germany).

ANWB (Dutch Tourist Board).

APPENDIX III – INSPECTION CHECK LIST

GENERAL

Barge name: ....

Vendor (name, address, phone): ....

Broker (name, address, phone): ....

Where seen: ....

OVERALL

Type...

Sailing rig..

Year built ....

Size

    Length..

    Beam ....

    Draft..

    Air draft (wheelhouse up)..

    Air draft (wheelhouse down)..

HULL

Overall condition...

Exterior pitting/rust ....

Extent of overplating/replating ....

Interior protection/rust...

Evidence of leaks ....

TOP

Shape (aesthetics, workability, efficiency)..

Material..

Condition ....

Windows ....

Wheelhouse ....

    Demountable (yes / no)..

INTERIOR

Condition ....

Finishes ....

Insulation ....

Type ....

Thickness ....

Damp ....

Layout ....

Accommodation provided (rooms, berths) ....

....

Headroom ....

Storage ....

Furniture ....

   Fixed ....

   Loose ....

Access for bulky items ....

Domestic equipment (list with type and condition of each) ......

....

....

Special features ....

....

EQUIPMENT

Engine room ....

Location ....

Access ....

   For people..

      From (outside / accommodation / wheelhouse) ....

      Type (door / hatch) ....

      Ease ....

   For equipment..

Space (headroom, crampedness)..

Protection from machinery ....

Walls...

Fire resistance ....

Insulated ....

Engine..

Type ....

Manufacturer...

Serial number ....

Year built ....

Capacity ....

Power ....

Number of cylinders ....

Maximum revolutions/minute ....

Current engine hours...

Rebuild...

Year...

Engine hours ....

By...

Scope of work..

Other repairs history ....

Condition...

Cooling type (air, raw water, indirect, skin tank, keel) ....

Exhaust ....

Type (wet / dry)..

Condition...

Engine instruments...

List...

Convenience ....

Mounts (solid / flexible) ....

Fuel supply ....

Tanks (number; size, material, and condition of each) ....

    Header tank (yes / no) ....

    Installation and filters ....

    Drive ....

Gearbox ....

    Manufacturer ....

    Type ....

    Serial number ....

    Reduction ....

    Rebuild ....

        Year ....

        Engine hours ....

        By ....

        Scope of work ....

Other repairs history ....

Propeller shaft ....

    Diameter ....

    Separate thrust bearing (yes / no) ....

    Universal joints (yes / no) ....

Propeller ....

    Material ....

    Number of blades ....

    Diameter ....

    Pitch ....

    Condition ....

    Bow thruster (yes / no) ....

        Type ....

        Condition ....

Navigation. ....

    Steering ....

    Type (chain or cable / manual hydraulic / powered hydraulic) ....

    Condition ....

Navigation instruments ....

    Lights ....

    Horn ....

    VHF radio ....

    Blue flag ....

    Other (compass, etc.) ....

Safety ....

    Escape exits ....

    Ability to shed water ....

    Water-tight bulkheads ....

    Fire extinguishers (number, type, certification) ....

    Bilge pumps (number, location, type) ....

Anchors ....

    Number, and for each ....

    Type ....

    Winch ....

    Length of chain ....

Systems. ....

    Domestic water ....

    Tanks (number; size, materials, and condition of each) ....

    Pumps (number, type of each) ....

    Plumbing ....

        Material ....

        Installation quality ....

    Insulation (yes / no) ....

    Water heating ....

    Heat source (engine waste heat, generator waste heat, oil, gas, other) ....

....

    Method (on demand or tank) ....

    Tank capacity ....

    Fixtures (list and location of each) ....

....

Waste water. ....

    Toilets (list; type, and location of each) ....

    Disposal method(s)..

Waste tanks (number; size, materials, and condition of each) ....

....

Waste pumps (number; capacity, type, and manufacturer of each)......................

....

Electricity. ....

Engine DC system ....

    Voltage..

    Battery ....

    Capacity ....

    Year installed ....

    Condition ....

    Charging methods..

    Capacity of each ....

Domestic DC system ....

    Voltage..

    Battery ....

    Capacity ....

    Year installed ....

    Condition ....

    Charging ....

Main engine alternator (yes / no, capacity)..

    Charger ....

    Manufacturer...

    Type (single stage, multi-stage, etc.) ....

    Capacity ....

DC Generator...

    Manufacturer...

    Capacity ....

    Cooling (air / water)...

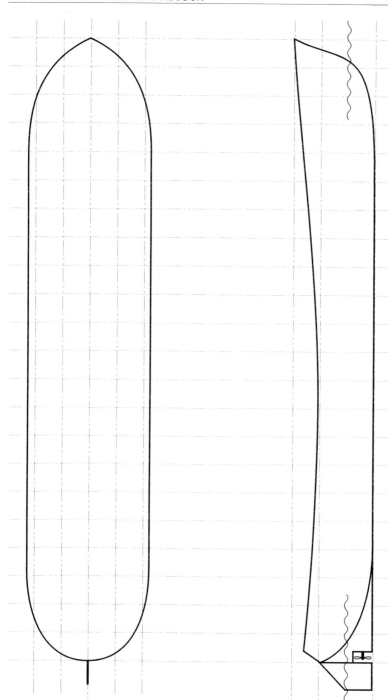

You may find it useful to draw a graph of your intended barge. This Illustration, in metre squares, shows plan and elevation for a klipper 22 m × 4.4 m. A plain graphs allows you to draw the basic dimensions of any barge. Photocopy and enlarge this blank as a first step.

The blank can then be filled in with the basic layout with particular notes or observations you may wish to refer to later, and relate to any photographs you have taken.

FOCSLE STORE
BUNK
CLOSET
SHOWER WC
SHELVES
SEAT
TABLE
SEAT
GALLEY
BUNK
CLOSET
DESK
WC
CLOSET
BUNK
CUPBOARD

GENERATOR STORE etc.
BUNK
TANK
SALOON
SEAT
GALLEY
TANKS
WHEELHOUSE
BUNK
BUNK
ENGINE
WC
TANK
BUNK

AIMS OF THE DUTCH BARGE ASSOCIATION

The DBA was launched at the London International Boat Show in January 1992.

Membership is open to anyone interested in any type of barge or similar vessel.

The Association aims to:

- Bring together people interested in barges.

- Link with other societies and clubs, and to establish contact with navigation authorities and trade associations at home and abroad.

- Represent barge owners' interests in areas such as mooring rights, navigational permits and charges, and safety regulations.

- Introduce owners and potential owners to professional advisers and institutions.

- Arrange regular meetings and social functions at which there will be the opportunity for members to learn more about barging in general and barge handling, maintenance, repairs and equipment in particular.

- Establish a register of owners, their barges and equipment, to enable members to share information.

- Publish a newsletter including articles on all aspects of barging from purchase and insurance to continental cruising. Contributions from members play a vital part in the newsletter's success.

- Seek commercial benefits for members in the form of discounts on the prices of barge-related goods and services.

MEMBERSHIP FEE - Please apply for current rates. Open to individual owners, prospective owners and those with an interest in these craft.

Overseas members are especially welcome.

For further information please contact the membership secretary:

DBA

Port Werburgh, Vicarage Lane Hoo, Rochester, Kent ME3 9TW

Tel: 07000 BARGES (07000 227437)

Fax: (01932) 765734

D.B.A.   MEMBERSHIP APPLICATION

NAME . . . .

ADDRESS . . . .

. . . .

County . . . . Post Code . . . .

OCCUPATION . . . .

TELEPHONE: Home . . . . Business . . . .

SHIP'S DETAILS

NAME . . . .

REGISTRATION NO . . . .

TYPE . . . . YEAR BUILT . . . .

LENGTH OVERALL . . . . BEAM . . . .

DRAFT . . . .

LENGTH ON WATERLINE . . . . AIR DRAFT . . . .

POWER SAIL . . . .

TYPE OF ENGINE(S) . . . .

GEARBOX . . . .

OTHER EQUIPMENT OF INTEREST . . . .

. . . .

. . . .

MOORING LOCATION (Medway/Thames etc.) . . . .

. . . .

FLAG . . . .

PRESENT CONFIGURATION (converted/unconverted) . . . .

. . . .

. . . .

PRESENT USAGE (Cruising/residential/charter) . . . .

. . . .

. . . . PTO.

BRIEF HISTORY

. . . .

. . . .

. . . .
. . . .
. . . .
. . . .
. . . .

GENERAL DETAILS

BOATING INTEREST . . . .
. . . .
. . . .
. . . .

HOW COULD THE DBA HELP YOU ? . . . .
. . . .
. . . .
. . . .

HOW COULD YOU HELP THE DBA ? . . . .
. . . .
. . . .
. . . .

Please consider me as a Private Member

I wish to pay a subscription of £ . . . . per annum by cheque

I wish to pay a subscription of £ . . . . by standing order

(Please check for current membership rates)

I understand that Membership or renewal may be declined at the discretion of the committee, without reason being given.

Signed. . . . .

Print name . . . .

Please return membership form to the DBA Membership Secretary at:

Port Werburgh, Vicarage Lane, Hoo, Rochester, Kent ME3 9TW